ON WET FOUNDATIONS
travel memoir

~

Kindle e-books by the same author

Thorny Acres
a novel set in an East Anglian village
*

Escargot Days
a novel set in France
*

They Called Her Miranda
a novel set in Malaysia
*

Brief Encounters - short story collection

PROLOGUE

Late October. The Canal du Bourgogne will be closing its gates next month and the lock keepers will get on with their winter lives until March. We have time for a leisurely cruise through the Ouche Valley before we coil our ropes and settle down for winter. The valley is at its most beautiful at this time of year. The sight of trees in their Autumn colours on the canal bank and hillsides beyond make my throat ache.

Peter is cooking supper on a bed of wood beside me; maybe our last barbecue this year. Wood smoke curls up and mingles with a canopy of bronze and gold above our heads. The little River Ouche flows gently before us and the evening sun casts a mellow glow on our home in the canal behind.

Soon the water will turn pink, then red, as it reflects another beautiful sunset. We will snuggle into warm jumpers, light the hurricane lamp and sit by the glow of dying wood embers until it becomes too chilly to sit beneath the trees. Meanwhile, enjoying the evening tranquillity, and the fact that my husband is cooking my supper, I sit and reflect on our time afloat.

Much water has passed under the bridge, both metaphorically and literally, since a ten franc coin changed our lives.

Chapter One

THREE SIDES TO A COIN

There was only one way to make a decision as important as this.

I tossed the coin.

Peter closed his eyes – coward! – and waited for the clatter of metal on table. In the ensuing silence, he opened his eyes and looked inquiringly up at the ceiling. I took his hand and pointed to where the ten franc piece had landed in a bowl of spaghetti bolognaise.

'Which way up is it?' Peter still wasn't looking.

'Narrow edge up.' I fished the coin out and licked tomato sauce off my fingers.

'Okay.' His head nodded while his lungs slowly expelled deeply drawn breath. 'I'll go for that.'

So we bought a sixty year old cargo barge.

To be honest, it wasn't *really* a heads we do, tails we don't situation anyway. It was more heads we do, tails we think about it a few more days before we do.

We had seen Colibri – once. We had explored her dark, cavernous hold. We had stood at the huge teak wheel covered in sixty years' worth of peeling varnish, looked down the boat's hatch board and tarpaulin covered length and said, 'How the hell do you *drive* a thing this size?'

Quite simply, we were in love. We had to have this boat. We were committed.

We told a friend of our plans. He shook his head in disbelief and said, 'I think you two should be committed!'

Maybe we should have been. After all, what did we know about barges? Peter is an aircraft engineer for heaven's sake! Sure, we'd had a fair amount of boating experience. I well remember being tipped out of a home made canoe when I was eight months pregnant. The baby survived – surprisingly, so did I – and we later taught him to sail in a twelve foot plastic dinghy. We did once build a twenty foot cabin cruiser in a lounge, but did that prepare us for building a lounge in an eighty seven foot barge?

The idea of converting and living on a canal barge had arrived as a bit of a shock anyway. We always thought we were going to live on a yacht at sea! For years we talked about doing this; had even progressed to forming positive plans. Peter would finish his current contract in Dubai then, after another two year contract elsewhere, we would buy our yacht and take a year out to sail. A sort of rehearsal, just to ascertain that it was what we both really wanted to do . . .

Flipping through *Yachting Monthly*, Peter announced, 'There's a Snowgoose catamaran called Tiger Lily for sale in Malta. I had my first ever boat in Malta.'

'I remember,' I replied. 'I got tipped out of it just before I had our first ever child in Malta.'

'We only had two children.'

'We only had three boats.'

'I know, it's time we had another one.'

'Peter, both our kids are in their twenties. I don't want another one.'

Peter sat dreaming about a year at sea. I sat remembering a year in Malta; the first year of our marriage. Our intrepid little dinghy sailor was born towards the end of that year, and he was . . . what? . . . twenty three now!

'Darling,' I said, as I slipped onto my husband's lap, 'do you realize it's our silver wedding anniversary next year?'

'Darling,' said my husband, as he slipped his hand under my bottom, retrieved *Yachting Monthly* and ran his hand tenderly over the crumpled pages, 'do you realize that would be an excellent year to buy a boat in Malta?'

He was joking of course. This simply was not the time to take a year off work to go sailing!

With our two parrots, we flew to Malta – I hasten to clarify that all four of us chose the Boeing method. Without our two parrots, we moved on board a Snowgoose catamaran called Tiger Lily.

Do not ever be lulled into thinking that you can take two

parrots into Malta armed with the volume of paperwork Malta has insisted on. They change their minds when parrots try to clear immigration!

The fact that Tiger Lily's interior had been constructed by a lunatic let loose with a Fisher Price tool kit concerned us less than the fact that our parrots were incarcerated at Luqa Airport.

We did have two sound hulls. The surveyor had been very positive about that – if sketchy about the interior. We wondered if we could expect to have two sound parrots.

We gave some consideration to Tiger Lily's engine. We considered that whoever installed a marinised Mk 2 Cortina engine in a boat had obviously never tried to start a Mk 2 Cortina on a damp morning. But, we intended to sail, with the engine as back up only – if we ever got our parrots out of custody.

When, under armed escort, our parrots were eventually delivered to the boat, our spirit of adventure was reinstated. We set sail, heading west.

How to describe the next few months? Briefly, I think. I could pass quickly over an eighteen hour storm, but I could linger over dolphins surrounding us in calm water and the sighting of land after three days at sea. Suffice it to say, it was exhilarating and exhausting. Interesting and terrifying. A never to be forgotten experience. Suffice it to say, the Mediterranean is a bitch!

I stayed with it for six months, wanting to get everything we could out of this trip. I was unlikely to repeat this rehearsal of our dream. If I am to be honest, I have to admit that my fondest memories of our ocean going sailing yacht are of two weeks tied up in Bizerte harbour in Tunisia and two months in the French canals.

August saw us on the coast of Majorca; listening to yet another gale warning from Radio Monaco. Out of deference to my impending nervous breakdown, we accepted that it was time to concede.

But we considered ourselves lucky. Albeit short lived, we had actually realized our dream – and the fact that God didn't design me to be a sailor! Day sailing, weekend sailing, in a flip flops and shorts climate without too much wind, fine. Not full time, live aboard, *doesn't this damn boat ever stay level!* sort of sailing.

We crossed to mainland Spain and headed for France. The idea being to take Tiger Lily through inland France to England. Motor sailing out of the Bay of Rosas and into the Gulf of Lyons, we heard the forecast for the Gulf of Lyons. Force ten – again!

In the dark, we dropped an anchor in Ceberes; the first French port over the border from Spain. After a few hours sleep, at about the time night was tentatively deciding to become day, we slipped out of harbour. Sails were hoisted into a nice fresh breeze as the sun was rising on what promised to become a perfect day. It kept its promise. In fact, we and Tiger Lily enjoyed one of the best day's sailing since we had been in the Mediterranean together.

None of us were fooled though. Radio Monaco does not lie. They sometimes get East and West and Tuesday and Thursday confused in the English translation, but they don't usually get breezes confused with gales. That force ten was going to happen, right where we were, in the early hours of Saturday. This was Thursday.

Late afternoon, we let down the sails, left the sea and turned into Port la Nouvelle. Next day, with the mast unstepped and lashed to the coach roof, we entered our first canal.

That's all we did. Passed under a bridge and entered the canal. We immediately tied the boat to some rings on the bank, opened our last cardboard carton of Spanish vino and ate a meal off plates that didn't need to be anchored to the table.

In the evening, the wind came. It whipped up dust and grit from the towpath into a cloud resembling a grubby desert sand storm. As the wind increased in ferocity, Tiger Lily reverberated like a semi congealed blancmange, the mooring ropes twanged like a badly tuned harp – and we slept like babies. Our first full, completely relaxed sleep for months.

Two days later, we plucked up courage to go through our first lock. Well, let's be honest here, trying to stuff a sixteen foot wide catamaran into a slightly more than sixteen foot wide lock can be a touch unnerving.

Our timing was lousy. It was late afternoon and, on approaching the dreaded lock, we saw a couple of dozen people standing around it. As we were to learn, locks attract people. This one was peopled by post siesta strollers, and they were in luck.

Adding to the attraction of staring into an empty lock, here was a boat coming to enter it.

Or was it?

It was obvious from the expressions on a couple of dozen faces that there was some doubt that a boat that wide would actually fit into a lock that narrow.

We were thinking: A boat this wide can't possibly fit into a lock that narrow!

And the last thing we needed right now was an audience!

I was aware of Peter's sharp intake of breath when the catamaran's two bows came within inches of the lock gates. As we slid smoothly into the lock, the expulsion of that breath was clearly audible. Like most of the spectators, I was still holding mine.

Nervously twisting a handful of rope that I wasn't quite sure what to do with, I heard an English voice: 'Well done! That looks rather difficult.'

'I suppose it is really,' I said, passing my bundle of rope to a bystander who did seem to know what to do with it. ' But you get used to it after a while.'

In the time it took for us to rise all of three feet, the bystander unravelled my cat's cradle and handed neat coils of rope back to me. To waves and calls of *bonne chance*, we bowed out of the lock, motored up to the next one and moored up for the night.

Three hundred and eighty five locks to Calais is a lot of locks. We didn't crunch a single one! We lost control of Tiger Lily in a huge Rhone lock, but we didn't hit any lock gates.

On arrival in Calais, we tied up just before the last lock that marked the end of our journey through France. In order to make Tiger Lily comfortable for the sea crossing, she was ballasted with sixty bottles of wine.

Thumping the gate with the port bow as we entered, we passed through the last French lock and into the tidal waters of the English Channel – or is it the French Channel at this end? Two months after leaving the Mediterranean, we were out at sea again.

By this time, we both knew the answer. We had been right about living afloat; it was definitely what we wanted to do – but not at sea in a thirty seven foot sailboat.

I suppose we could say that Colibri was conceived on our wedding day – our silver wedding day – at Vandenesse, just before the summit of the Canal de Bourgogne.

Late September, halfway through France, we were already totally besotted with France and her rivers and canals. We were hooked on the relaxation and freedom of a newly discovered way of life. Beautiful scenery had unfolded before us and some delightful people had crossed our path.

Whilst in a lock on our way to Vandenesse, an elderly English lady from another boat came to talk to Peter. She wore a large floppy hat and a long dress, and she carried a bunch of wild flowers. Just before I interrupted their conversation by saying: 'Excuse me, I'm sorry to interrupt, but I think you ought to know, Peter, our engine seems to be on fire', I had been thinking that I would love to be a dotty English lady wandering the canal banks and picking wild flowers – for something like . . . maybe . . . the rest of my life.

We were tired by the time we reached Vandenesse. Twenty locks had been accomplished that day; not bad when taking into account time out to deal with a minor fire before it became major. At the lock before Vandenesse, we were given a sizeable sheaf of papers. These told us, in three different languages, that the next eight locks were autonomous. Basically, this meant we had to operate them ourselves, without the assistance of a lock keeper. Copious writing, diagrams and pictures of little match stick men propelling matchstick rafts with matchstick oars were provided for our guidance.

'Looks like fun,' I said, flexing my weary lock gate opening muscles. 'Let's rest here for the night.'

The evening was warm. We cast ropes over a couple of bollards and ate our evening meal ashore at a thoughtfully provided log table. Afterwards, we spread the match stick men illustrated lock operating instruction pages out – probably what the log table had been thoughtfully provided for – and reflected on how much nicer French vin de table was than cardboard Spanish vino. By that time, we had discovered the five franc a litre bottles with stars on.

Faced with a challenging day of eight do- it- yourself locks and two miles of tunnel to negotiate, we cast off soon after eight next morning. Clutching an armful of empty stared litre bottles, I strode purposefully to the lock to do my autonomous bit; and encountered a couple of problems.

There was no rubbish bin for my bottles – and there was a thumping great boat in the lock!

It wasn't just a boat. It was a barge. A beautiful, shiny, black and red barge, with windows in the side and flower tubs on deck. I fired questions at the English driver of the barge:

'Is it yours?' – 'What sort of barge is it?' – 'Did you convert it yourself?' – 'Where are you going?'

He obligingly answered all my questions in the time it took for the barge to sink down in the lock: 'Yes, it's mine.' – 'She's a Dutch cargo barge.' – 'Yes, I did the conversion.' – 'I'm going South to spend winter in the Canal du Midi.'

He then threw in some questions of his own: 'Is that your Snowgoose out there?' – 'Been in the Med. have you?' – 'Thought so. I spent a season in the Med. on a Snowgoose, that's why I've got this barge now.' – 'You're not going to throw those bottles away are you? There's a franc refund on each one of those.'

I helped him open the lock gates, then ran onto the bridge to yell down at Peter: 'Hey! I've found it. I've found what we . . .'

'I know. I can see it.' He yelled back.

It was a glorious tee shirt and shorts September day. The locks were a mere few hundred yards apart, and there was nothing to this business of operating them yourself – except exhaustion!

A blissful morning. Could there possibly be a nicer way to spend the day that marked the anniversary of twenty five years of marriage?

I wandered along the sunny towpath, preparing locks for Peter to drive into and trying to recall how many returnable one franc bottles we had binned. Under a clear blue sky, birds sang in the trees, dragonflies skimmed the water, their beautiful turquoise wings glinting in the sunlight, and a mad man in a lock cottage shouted at about fourteen cats. Well, there may not have been as many as fourteen; he was chasing them out of the cottage with a broom, and some went back in through a window and may well have been chased out again.

A beautiful day ended with another warm, balmy evening and an idyllic mooring by an old stone bridge in the middle of nowhere. To celebrate our special day, we had a shower, opened a bottle of vin de pays and enjoyed a barbecue on the bank under trees.

Peter gave me a silver ten franc coin.

Snuggled contentedly together, we sat under the stars and talked about the barge we had seen that morning. Maybe . . . one day . . . when I've been back to work for a couple of years, sort of talk.

Nine months later, we tossed my silver ten franc coin, found that it had three sides, and we were delivered of a barge.

Chapter Two

A BARGE IS BORN

It wasn't supposed to happen so soon. We had planned to wait a few years. We tried to fight it, really we did, but Malcolm kept 'phoning and trying to make us go to Belgium.

Hearing a telephone ring was unnerving anyway. Although we had been living on Tiger Lily for less than a year, we had adapted to life without telephones, televisions and Hoovers. We hadn't, however, adapted to cold weather and, with winter on the near horizon, we vacated Tiger Lily and moved ourselves and the parrots into plug in switch on hot and cold running bricks and mortar civilization. I was happy to be reunited with the washing machine – the only electrical appliance I had seriously missed – and we settled into central heated hibernation.

Tiger Lily was craned out of the water and put on storage blocks. Our decision of whether or not to sell her now . . . later . . . at all, was also put into storage. She had been our home for months and we had been through some rough and some good times together. She had brought us safely through an unforgettable phase in our lives and, in our era of geriactricity, when senile gums have trouble chewing custard and anything more solid is passed by courtesy of Senacot, we will feed on memories of places seen and people encountered. Apart from anything else, it was something we just had to do, and will be forever glad that we did.

We hadn't been exposed to a cold climate for several years, and England in winter held little appeal. Mother donated a thermal vest and Marks and Spencers matched it. I was shocked by the price of thermal vests! We hoped it would not be too long before Peter found new overseas employment. His sabbatical year was nearly up and he was practising saying, 'W – w – work.' I was practising what to say to the bank manager if Peter didn't find w – w – work soon.

Peter contacted some people in the aviation industry, bought Flight International and read the Sits. Vac. column. I bought *Waterways World* and read about narrow boats and canals in summer.

Our daughter 'phoned from Berlin to ask what she should send us for Christmas. She wasn't sure that she could buy thermal vests in Berlin.

A telephone call came from Qatar. Would Peter go and work on some helicopters for two weeks? Yes, he certainly would; especially as the possibility of a longer term contract was also mentioned.

'Not fair,' I grumbled as I packed Peter's shorts and flip flops. 'You get two weeks of Middle East sunshine, while I get two weeks of scraping ice off a windscreen so I can go and stand in a queue at Tescos.'

Tension threatened to destroy my equilibrium on the drive to Heathrow Airport. Being left hand drive, our jeep was not conducive to relaxed motoring in Britain. It didn't seem to bother Peter, but it sure as hell bothered me being in the right hand seat without a steering wheel and brake pedal! On the M25, I thought of an article I once read about menopausal American women hyperventilating. I wasn't actually sure what this meant, but I believe I was just about to find out when my reflexes snapped into safety alert and I averted hyperventilation and premature menopause by screaming at Peter.

'Peter! For heaven's sake, SLOW DOWN!'

'But, Meg, I'm only doing seventy miles an hour!'

'Okay! Sorry! Watch that truck, it's going to pull out!'

'Meg, please just . . .'

'Right, I'll shut up.'

I tried to, really I did, but it wasn't easy. I just simply wasn't coping with being shut in a car that, vying with other cars and lorries for space, was travelling at more than cycling speed. Easing my white knuckled grip on the seat belt, I attempted to take an equally strong grip on my frayed nerves; assuring myself that I would re- adapt to this normal pace of life soon enough.

I didn't adapt quite soon enough to cope brilliantly well with driving myself back from Heathrow. I did manage, quite easily really, to find the right car on the right floor of the right car park. Even found my way through the parking payment procedure. Negotiating a large roundabout onto the M25 wasn't as difficult as it looked and, gaining confidence, I accelerated and moved into the middle lane.

It was the exit sign to Farnborough that alerted me to the fact that I was travelling in the wrong direction. I had heard stories of people driving round the M25 for hours – days even – trying to get off. I had hitherto assumed they were just silly people in silly stories!

It took me rather longer to drive back than it had taken Peter to drive there. Brentwood High Street, between five and six o'clock on a Friday evening, isn't much fun I promise you. At about the time Peter was flying over Kuwait, I was arriving back in Ipswich; my fingers and shoulders aching from tensely gripping the steering wheel for hours.

Shaky with relief, I went indoors, kicked off my shoes and, clutching a half pint tumbler of one of France's fuller bodied red wines, slumped thankfully into a stationary chair. Using one hand to steady the other, I raised the tumbler to my lips.

The telephone rang, my hands flew in the air and the tumbler landed in my lap – it was no longer full, and I was red bodied as I grabbed the nerve jangling telephone.

'Could I speak to Peter please?' asked an unfamiliar voice.

'Sorry, he's not here. He'll be away until the 12th.'

'Oh dear. I've been ringing all day; I was hoping he would go and do some work for us in Belgium.'

'Where?'

'Belgium. Perhaps you would ask him to call Malcolm as soon as he gets back?'

When Peter called from Qatar, I told him that Malcolm wanted to speak to him. He said, 'Who?'

'Malcolm. He wants you to go to Belgium.'

'Where?'

'Belgium.'

Peter called again a few days later to say he was staying in Qatar a further two weeks, and the prospect of a two year contract was looking good.

The morning of the 12th, Malcolm 'phoned. 'Is Peter back yet?'

'I'm afraid not. Another two weeks.'

'Ah! Could you please get him to call me as soon as he gets back? This Belgium thing is rather urgent. We need an engineer out there soon.'

'I will certainly give Peter your message,' I assured Malcom. 'But, actually, he is looking for work overseas.'

'Belgium is overseas.'

'Well yes, I suppose it is, but I think he has more in mind a bit further over a bit more seas, if you see what I mean. Somewhere the sun shines quite often really.'

'If you could just ask him to call me?'

'Sure. As soon as he gets back.'

After a month, I was anxious to have Peter home. We decided it would be altogether less traumatic if British Rail delivered him from Heathrow, and the evening he was due to arrive, I waited for him to call from Ipswich station.

The telephone rang – why does it still make me jump so!

'Is he back yet?' asked Malcom.

'The day after tomorrow,' I lied.

That evening, over supper and what was left of the full bodied French stuff, Peter told me about Qatar. He talked of some super calm sea sailing and how the decision on the two year contract would be made when the Chief Engineer returned from leave.

I told Peter that I hated his tan and that a telegram had arrived from Oman asking him to go for an interview for a job in Muscat. 'Oh, and by the way, Malcolm wants you to call him about Belgium.'

'Why on earth would I want to go to Belgium?' Peter asked. 'When and where is the Oman interview?'

'Friday – as in tomorrow. At some hotel near Heathrow.'

Back to Heathrow. Peter drove. I waited in an hotel lounge, thumbing through *Waterways World,* whilst two Arabs talked to Peter in a room somewhere. I tore an advertisement out of *Waterways World* and tucked it into my bag.

'Well?' I asked when Peter re- emerged. 'Is there a job?'

'Yes, there's a job. Yes, it's mine if I want it. No, we're not going to Muscat.'

Apparently, the two Arabs told Peter that there was a very good social life in Muscat. Peter asked about the work. They spoke of it vaguely and said that the social life was very good. Peter asked about the aircraft he would be expected to work on. They didn't seem to know too much about the aircraft, but they knew that the social life was good. Peter asked about the salary. They said that the Company housing was of a high standard and the social life was excellent. Peter asked again about the salary, then shook hands with the Arabs before walking towards the door. They asked Peter to let them know when he had reached a decision. Peter told them that he had already decided he couldn't afford a social life on the salary they were offering.

There was an air of despondency as we drove home. The M25 in lashing rain is no more fun than Brentwood High Street between five and six o'clock on a Friday. Shouting above thrashing windscreen wipers, we reviewed the situation so far.

Peter didn't know when he would hear about Qatar, the Oman was definitely out and nothing else of interest had manifested itself. As we sat at red traffic lights behind a hundred and one dripping cars in Brentwood High Street at half past five, I said, 'Maybe you should talk to Malcolm?'

'Think I'll hang on for a bit,' Peter replied. 'I mean, why on *earth* would we want to go to Belgium?'

Next morning, I was washing up when Peter answered the telephone.

'Ah. Hello Malcolm. My wife told me you'd called.'

I closed the kitchen door.

A few minutes later, Peter opened the kitchen door and announced that, if Qatar hadn't contacted him by Sunday, he'd probably go to Belgium on Monday.

'Why on earth do you want to go to Belgium?' I asked.

'Because,' Peter explained, 'it would only be for two or three weeks. Just to help them out of a fix. Meanwhile, they'll arrange a posting to somewhere the sun shines quite often.' Apparently, this company dealt in aviation contracts all over the world.

Peter went to Belgium Monday morning. Qatar telephoned Monday evening. I said that Peter was no longer available as he had gone to Belgium. They said, 'Where?' I said, 'BELGIUM!'

I didn't bother to mention that it was only for two or three weeks.

After seven weeks, we had become quite fond of Belgium. The

first couple of weeks, Peter came home to visit me. He flew into Southend Airport on a Company 'plane and I drove to Southend to pick him up. The flight from Brussels took about an hour. Peter reckoned that the drive from Ipswich to Southend would take about an hour. So, the first Sunday, I got into the car at about the time Peter boarded his 'plane.

Peter was wrong! Okay, so he knew about flight times – but he sure as hell knew nothing about the late Sunday afternoon traffic on the A12!

Half an hour after leaving home, I crawled along the inside lane in second gear, beside a grey Ford Fiesta that had become a familiar sight in the outside lane beside me. Frustration and near panic were mounting. I would be late for Peter and I was trapped in a hot metal container, shrouded in petrol and diesel fumes, with no means of escape.

I had tried, but I was just not adapting to normal life. Instead, I was becoming more and more paranoid about noise, fumes, traffic and junk mail.

Lighting a cigarette to steady my nerves, I slipped into third gear. Brief exhilaration of speed and back down to second gear. The lady in the grey Ford Fiesta looked at me and shrugged. Two and a half miles on, a child and a Dalmatian got out of a Volvo three cars ahead of me. The Dalmatian cocked its leg against a hub cap two cars ahead of me and the child peed behind a no parking sign. I exchanged smiles with the lady in the grey Ford Fiesta.

The outside lane accelerated into third gear and the lady waved goodbye from her grey Ford Fiesta. I waved back as I crept past the Fiesta a mile later. When she drew alongside me at the Hatfield Peveral turn off, Joan – well, she looked like a Joan, and I felt we had known each other long enough to be on Christian name terms – grinned at me through the windscreen of her grey Ford Fiesta. Together, we limped on to Chelmsford.

Parting company with Joan and her Fiesta at the Army and Navy roundabout, I picked up speed and reached Southend Airport forty five minutes after Peter landed.

The following Sunday, with my timing carefully planned, I picked up the car keys and braced myself for the A12. I jumped when the telephone rang. It was a fellow engineer of Peter, with a message that Peter would be delayed. President Reagan was due to fly into Brussels, and all flights were held back until the President's 'plane had landed.

Great! That was all I needed on top of the A12 on a Sunday afternoon – President bloody Reagan effing up my schedule!

Surely it would be easier for me to visit Peter?

Because he was there only temporarily, Peter stayed in a small hotel in Zaventem; a few miles from the Airport. I was supposedly living in Ipswich with the parrots, but I more and more exercised my visiting rights and spent as much time as I could with Peter.

I loved Zaventem in spring. There was something soft and gentle about this little Belgian town, and I always experienced a feeling of warmth and contentment when I stepped off the train at Zaventem station.

One morning, as I left the station, a sweet little girl, about seven years old, ran up to me and began speaking in Flemish. I smiled, shook my head and walked on. The little girl trotted along beside me, jabbering away. I stopped, smiled and said, 'Sorry, love, I don't understand you, I'm English.'

'Oh shit!' said the sweet little girl and stomped off in disgust.

Still smiling, I raised my face to the sun and, with "Doh a Deer, a Female Deer" gently oozing from speakers along the street, I continued my short walk to the hotel in the square.

The hotel was fun. It was owned by Madame; a charming lady who rapidly delivered strangely punctuated English accompanied by extravagant gestures involving full use of both arms. A sort of verbose Flemish windmill. Madame was assisted in the general running of the hotel by a multi purpose, all black Zairian lad called Theodore, who always greeted me with: 'Good morning, Madame,' when I 'phoned Peter in the evenings. Whenever I arrived at the hotel – which I did with increasing regularity – Theodore would beam radiantly, shake my hand and tell me how nice it was to see me again. I grew really fond of Theodore, and we came to love this slightly bizarre hotel.

The first room Peter occupied was on the top floor. The walls of this room were totally smothered in purple paper hosting huge yellow flowers which jostled each other for space. This affliction spread across the ultra high ceiling and precipitated migraine if observed for too long whilst reclining on the orange candlewick bedspread. An enormous radiator with bulging ribs was easier to hear than see amongst the vividly coloured horticultural display. It wasn't till my third visit that I spotted a framed print of Van Gogh's Sunflowers on a wall.

Peter often worked at night and I would take the night ferry from Felixtowe. It felt a bit like having an affair. Peter usually left the jeep outside the station for me, with a note on the front seat saying: 'Hi. Room number so and so today.' We met in the hotel room, where Peter would already be in bed and, of course, what with travelling all night, I would be ready to jump into bed at ten in the morning without even feeling decadent.

Well, I did feel decadent really. It was lovely!

Although she never charged for double occupancy, Madame told me that she always arranged for my husband to have a room with a double bed for when I visited him. I'm not sure she believed we were married. I hated to disillusion her by telling her we were.

Seven weeks moved into ten weeks. Whatever happened to: 'Two, maybe three weeks before we post you to somewhere the sun shines quite often'?

Who cared? The sun was shining that year, and Zaventem in summer was as delightful as Zaventem in spring. Did we really want to go somewhere hot and either humid or dusty dry? Before winter hit us, certainly, but for now, Peter was enjoying his work here. The salary matched the one Qatar would have offered if they had been able to make up their minds – and the social life was very pleasant.

Belgium is ever so close to Holland. The Monday of Peter's fifteenth temporary week, I said, 'We're so close, why don't we drive to Holland and look at some barges?'

'Because,' replied Peter, 'we have no idea where to look.'

I scrabbled in my bag and produced a crumpled advertisement torn out of *Waterways World*. 'See?' I flourished the scrap of paper. 'There's a telephone number of a guy who sells barges in a place called Enkhuizen. Mind you, he's probably sold all his barges by now, I found this advert in February.'

'You could give him a ring,' Peter suggested.

I gave him a ring. He had sold the barges in the advert, but he said he had some others. He could show us a clipper aak, two luxe motors and – I thought he said – some chollops.

We thought we may as well go and have a look. Just out of curiosity. Those clipper luxe chollop things were probably nothing like that barge we saw at Vandenesse. But, being so close, why not go and check out this barge business? After all, what was the point in spending the next couple of years in Malaysia or somewhere, dreaming of coming back to buy a barge, only to discover that it was a lousy idea?

Yes, we would drive to Holland tomorrow; probably take one look and realize instantly just what a lousy idea it was. Then we could put the whole idea out of our minds and settle down.

Altogether, a really excellent plan – which failed the minute we set eyes on Colibri!

We found the Barge Agent's office on the pretty water front at Enkhuizen. 'My name is Anna,' the tall, thin Dutch man announced as he shook our hands. 'First, I want to show you a barge that is nearby.'

We followed him along the sunlit water front where an assortment of smartly painted and varnished boats, looking rather splendid in this charming setting, made me doubt the validity of coming here to get this whole idea out of our system. Peter and I dawdled along, gazing in admiration at these super boats, wondering which of these beauties we were being taken to view.

Anna marched purposefully past the spectacular line up of smartly painted boats and stopped beside a big black hulk that reared up out of the reeds.

Cobwebs draped a chipped anchor hanging drunkenly from a battle scared bow. An old car tyre was suspended on a frayed rope from a rusty bollard. Faded, stained tarpaulin covered the cargo hold. I imagined rats nesting beneath it. The vessel was a scruffy heap of iron, but it somehow had a familiar look about it.

Feeling slightly stunned, I turned to look at Peter. He took my hand and squeezed it, and I knew he was feeling the same sense of shock that was rippling through me. He cleared his throat and asked, 'What is it?'

'A Luxe Motor,' said Anna.

So, now we knew. That boat we had fallen in love with at

Vandenesse wasn't just a barge – it was a Luxe Motor.

We explored the barge – after overcoming the difficulty of getting me on board. Being empty, the boat was very high above water level.

'Let me help.' Anna offered his hand. I put my hand in his. No, he wanted please my foot. In a manner that seriously endangered my dignity, I was man handled by Peter and Anna onto the side deck.

'A few tons of ballast will sort her out,' Anna declared.

'I beg your pardon!'

'He's talking about the boat,' Peter explained.

'The name of the boat is that of a little bird,' Anna enlightened us as he flapped back a corner of the faded tarpaulin then removed a heavy wooden hatch board. Peter still swears he saw a disturbed rat falling out of its clogs as it scurried away. By means of a very steep ladder, we climbed down into the cargo hold.

It was full of junk! Lumps of metal, a dozen or so stainless steel water tanks, piles of wood and boxes of assorted paraphernalia littered the vast wooden floor. It looked like a garage sale organised by a lunatic who hoped a Fisher Price tool kit would sell unnoticed amongst this lot.

Easing my way round two huge lumps of machinery bolted to the floor, I ran my hands over the ribbed and rivetted iron wall. This thing was built like a battle ship!

Blinking like bemused moles, we climbed back up the long ladder and re- emerged into daylight. Following Anna's sure footed lead, I edged my way cautiously along the side deck until we reached what appeared to be an over the top Kew Gardens green house.

'This,' our intrepid guide informed us, 'is the wheel house.' After fighting our way through a jungle of head threatening pot plants, we descended steep steps into the aft living quarters.

'Did the bargee *and* his family actually live in here?' I asked.

'The children would have slept in the forepeak,' Anna told me.

'You mean there's more?'

'Come, I'll show you.'

Back through the David Bellamy jungle terrain, down the long side deck to the front of the barge. My legs ached, and I still had to climb through a hatch and down again into a funny little room.

Two miniature bunks, some tucked away cupboards, a tiny table and narrow seats were cleverly built into this weird shaped area that tapered off into the bow of the ship. It was easy to imagine that Lewis Carroll had been here before he introduced Alice to the pill habit.

After lunch and a pause for breath, we looked at two other barges. A Clipper Aark that was already converted; superbly so to an extremely high standard. The "chollops" turned out to be tjalks, and we looked at one of those. A gorgeous boat of the smartly painted and varnished variety, with a round bulbous bow and lee boards. Mouth wateringly beautiful.

Tired, dusty and mentally disturbed, we drove back to Zaventem.

We didn't talk much on the drive back. Amsterdam Ring Road between five and six o'clock on a Tuesday evening is only slightly more fun than the M25. Peter concentrated on the traffic and road signs whilst I tried to sort out the confusion in my brain.

Before driving through Antwerp, which is a case of Brentwood High Street eat your heart out, at any time, we stopped for something to eat at a motorway service area somewhere near Breda.

'Did you see those two air cooled generators?' asked Peter, pushing chips around his plate.

I turned to look round the cafeteria. 'I can't see any generators.'

'On that barge we looked at.'

'Which barge? We looked at three.'

'The first one.'

'Oh, that one. What generators?'

'Bolted to the floor. Damn great things. You know, Meg, we should have waited till we got back to Belgium to eat. The Dutch don't know how to make chips.'

He was right of course. Belgian frites are probably unsurpassed anywhere in the world – except possibly Dubai.

Back in the car, we started to talk a bit; about how strange it was that, in spite of the fact that Belgian potatoes are awful, their chips are wonderful. Pity they don't do fish and chips. We went on to reminisce about the best fish and chips ever. An enterprising Indian, who had experienced English fish and chips and, more importantly, English attitudes to fish and chips, opened a shop in

Dubai. He was run off his feet serving this precious delicacy, wrapped in especially imported copies of The Sun and Daily Mirror, to British ex patriots. None of us had ever eaten fish'n'chips as good in Britain.

Back at the hotel, a shower in the Belgian hip bath disposed of cobwebs from hair, grime from fingernails and some of our fatigue. Feeling refreshed, we sat up in bed drinking coffee and chatting about how pretty the little town of Enkhuizen is and how nice Anna the agent was before, tired from a long day, we settled down to sleep.

'It's no good, you know.' Twenty minutes later I prodded Peter's back. 'We've got to talk about this.'

'I know.' He sat up and switched on the bedside light. 'But where do we start?'

Once started, we couldn't stop.

'You liked that barge didn't you?'

'Yes. So did you!'

'Well?'

'Well what?'

'What are we going to do about it?'

'Make an offer I suppose.'

'What about our plans to earn some money in the sunshine?'

'We could scrap them. Shall I make some more coffee?'

'Or we could go ahead with those plans and buy a barge in a few years time. No, open a bottle of wine.'

'But we wouldn't be able to have *that* barge. Someone else will buy it.'

'There must be other barges.'

'Of course; there's bound to other barges.' Peter excused himself and left the room to visit the toilet on the floor below.

'We could look for another one,' he continued when he returned and caught me flushing the en- suite bidet. 'In a few year's time.'

'But you liked that one didn't you?'

'Yes. So did you.'

'You want that one, don't you?'

'Yes. So do you.'

'Well?'

'Well what?'

'Well, let's buy it. Come on, we both know we're going to.'

By the time we eventually went to sleep in the early hours of morning, we had mentally unbolted two damn great generators, put a comfortable lounge in their place and were cruising France in a barge called Colibri – the name of a little bird.

Chapter Three

ARE WE READY FOR THIS?

Cruising to England next day on a P & O Ferry called The Pride of Suffolk, I had six hours to think. That night, alone in bed, I couldn't sleep; got up to drink tea and did some more thinking. Hours later, sleepless but sensible, I got wise. I chickened out. I bottled it!

In the morning, I phoned the hotel. Theodore said, 'Good evening,' and I asked to speak to Peter. After I had assured Theodore that yes, I was well and yes, I would be returning soon, he fetched Peter to the telephone.

I said, 'HelloDarlingwecan'tdothisit'scrazyit'stoosoon - quick gulp of air - we're not ready to take this on yet we have to sell Tiger Lily before we can even think of buying another boat we don't know where we'll be this time next year we may be in Timbucwhatsit for all we know and what if we've lumbered ourselves with two boats . .

Jumping in quickly during a pause for breath, Peter said: 'Hang on. Calm down. If you're that worried, we'll cancel it all.'

'What? You mean cancel buying that barge because I'm worried?'

'Yes, there's no point in going ahead if it's upsetting you. Anyway, you're absolutely right. I'll 'phone Anna .'

'Thank you, I love you.'

'I've also had a chance to think sensibly since you left. Come back soon won't you?'

For various reasons, ten days elapsed before P & O delivered me back to Belgium on their daytime sailing. Arriving at Zaventem station in the evening, I was pleased to find Peter waiting. He greeted me with: 'I'm glad you're here, I'm starving.'

We headed for our favourite restaurant. The Italian Papa; head waiter and head of the family that made eating Italian food in an Italian atmosphere possible in a Belgian town, greeted us at the door and showed us to the tree shaded, walled garden. Even on this warm summer evening, the Signor wore a ruffle fronted shirt and bow tie and a dinner jacket that emitted a faint aroma of mothballs. Pizza margarita and spaghetti bolognaise were delivered to our check clothed, candle enhanced table with the aplomb one might expect from a head waiter at Maxims.

I raised my glass of house red and said, 'Shame about that barge.'

'Yes. Sensible decision though,' said Peter. 'Just as well we jumped on it before we got too enthusiastic.'

'Just think, what if we *had* gone ahead then you got posted to Timbucwhatsit!'

'I have thought.' He lowered a forkful of spaghetti before it reached his mouth. 'What if we had asked that agent chap, Emma . . .'

'Anna.'

'Well what if we asked him if it's possible to store a barge for a couple of years?'

'Hmm.'

'I mean, prices could - almost certainly will - go up over the next year or two.'

'Hmm.' I reached over and laid my hand on his - the constant stirring of spaghetti round a plate was beginning to irritate me.

'And then, Meg, there's no guarantee that we'd find a barge we like as much as we like this one.' He looked at me expectantly.

I tried being practical by pointing out that it takes about six weeks to buy a house. We had no idea how long it took to buy a barge. How would we manage if we left Belgium whilst it was all happening?

'Malcom phoned, as it happens,' Peter said. 'He asked if I would be prepared to stay here another two months. Apparently this contract finishes then anyway.'

'What then?'

'Who knows? But then, who knows anything?'

This was true of course. We hadn't known we would come to Belgium. We didn't know we would still be there six months later. We'd had no way of knowing we would fall in love with the first barge we looked at.

Let's face it, we didn't even know Malcom this time last year!

'All this is Malcom's fault,' I said.

'Not completely,' Peter pointed out. 'He wasn't responsible for the fact that we left Malta to sail the Mediterranean and ended up in the French canals.'

'No, that was Radio Monaco's fault.'

This was getting silly. Here we were, sitting over a half eaten pizza, trying to blame someone else for the fact that we had fallen in love with a bloody barge! Of course it was no one's fault - was it?

'You know what, Peter? Some one or something has put us here.'

'You did, Meg, it was you who said let's go to the Italian restaurant.'

'No, stupid, I mean we shouldn't be here at all! We never meant to come to Belgium. We actually fought against it. I mean, if Qatar had phoned a day earlier, we wouldn't even have gone to Enkhuizen. And why was Colibri just sitting there that day, waiting for us; the first damn barge we ever looked at? It seems like . . . well . . . it's like something is directing us against our will or something. I mean . . . oh blast it, I don't really know what I do mean!'

'Well then, don't call *me* stupid,' said Peter. 'At least I know what you mean. Things seem to be so much out of our control, we might as well toss a coin!'

From the depths of my bag, came the silver ten franc coin.

'You toss it,' said Peter, closing his eyes. 'I don't want to be responsible for this.'

A drive to Enkhuizen. Just to take a second look and make sure we really did want to buy this barge.

We really did want to buy this barge.

We didn't know quite what to do with two thumping great air cooled generators that, on second inspection, we found were not merely bolted, but actually welded to the iron floor supports. Somehow, we would have to remove them from our future sitting room.

Whilst we were pondering this problem, Anna left us to go above to talk to a man who had just arrived on deck. Anna returned and informed us that the man had made an offer for the generators. Colibri's price was instantly reduced accordingly, and arrangements were made for the generators' new owner to remove the offending equipment.

With that problem out of the way, we paid a deposit and agreed to buy Colibri subject to survey.

'A good decision,' Anna told us. 'My storage cost is not high, and in two years time you would pay much higher for a barge such as this.'

Typical agent talk, of course, but we were to discover in later years that he was right. We discovered in the next few weeks that he was a pleasure to do business with. In fact, once we had overcome the difficulty of making up our minds, Anna made the whole process of buying our barge quite easy for us. He arranged for the boat to come out of the water, engaged a surveyor, advised us of the survey date and told us we could be present to talk to the surveyor

On the appointed day, we drove to Enkhuizen to find Colibri already slipped and looking like a huge beached whale. Boats always look different out of water - they look bigger.

Feeling about the size of an autonomous lock matchstick man, I gazed up at Colibri in awe.

'Wow!' I said.

'Double wow!' said Peter. 'That's one helluva lot of boat to paint!'

Someone had played noughts and crosses on Colibri's belly - except, there didn't seem to be any noughts in the Dutch version of the game. The chalk crosses marked the findings of the surveyor's ultra sonic test equipment. Some areas of the hull were below required thickness and would have to be replated. This was apparently normal in a barge this age, and not our problem because the vendor pays.

Had the noughts been chalked in, they would have won the game. Our newly acquired hull was a solid bit of Dutch Iron shipbuilding of the 1930's era.

Once the replating had been completed to the surveyor's satisfaction and the hull twice tarred, we paid the balance of the agreed purchase price. Anna's job was now finished, but his interest wasn't. He took time to discuss our plans for the boat and to offer advice. We intended to do the interior conversion work ourselves, but replacing the wooden hatch boards with a hefty steel roof was, we knew, definitely beyond the capabilities of one man and his wife.

Anna obtained an estimate for the steel work and arranged for Colibri to be taken to the ship yard where the work would be carried out.

We felt rather like parents of a premature baby. Our friendly agent had delivered our barge and offered advice on her wellbeing. She was then transferred to Leeuwarden in Friesland for specialist treatment. She was sort of in an incubator for a while, being nursed into a condition that we could deal with ourselves. Meanwhile, all we could do was visit her.

Ridiculously excited, we drove to Leeuwarden to spend a weekend on board. This peculiar boat was actually ours, and we could explore and poke around to our hearts' content. I walked up, down and around our barge with a silly grin on my face; still trying to believe that we had really bought this baby.

We camped in the aft crew quarters, ate makeshift meals cooked on an antique two ring gas affair and drank wine out of coffee mugs. Plans for the steel work were discussed with the ship yard, and we measured the cargo hold so we could make plans for the interior conversion. Our first plan, however, was to sweep a film of orange metal grinding dust from the side deck. It clogged our shoes and was carted with us wherever we walked.

Arriving back in Zaventem late Sunday evening, we popped into the bar across the square to rinse our dusty throats before hitting the Belgian hip bath. In response to the warm greeting: 'Where the devil have you two been? You're filthy!' we offered the explanation that we had been to Holland for a dirty weekend.

That weekend was repeated as often as Peter was able to get away. We didn't bother to repeat the exercise of sweeping orange dust. It was pointed out to us that the men were always "*grin-ding*" and we would not be without this orange dust problem until Colibri left the ship yard.

Notwithstanding a floor permanently encrusted with *grin-ding* dust, bit by bit, the aft quarters became less grubby and more homely. We propped a mattress on a makeshift wooden frame and attached broom handles to the ceiling to act as a wardrobe.

Peter usually uses the bedroom floor as a wardrobe. After driving to Leeuwarden straight from work one Friday, Peter changed his clothes and, true to form, ignored the broom handles. Picking up his clothes to introduce them to a hanger, I wondered at the bulge in his trousers. As any wife would, I investigated, then asked: 'Peter, why have you got an egg in your pocket?'

'That's one of Theodore's eggs,' he replied.

'Okay. Why have you got Theodore's egg in your pocket?'

The explanation was quite straightforward really. It seems that the airport workers staying in the hotel often go on duty early in the morning; before the scheduled breakfast time. So, before going to bed, Theodore left flasks of coffee, slices of cheese in a clingfilm membrane and hard boiled eggs. The guys would drink the coffee, eat the cheese and put the eggs in their pockets for later.

Poor Theodore. Finding only empty flasks and discarded plastic membranes to clear away, he probably went back to Zaire and told the natives that English men eat egg shells.

One weekend, we found a network of steel angle beams where wooden hatchboards had once reclined. The boards were piled up on the quay side with the faded brown tarpaulin neatly folded on top. I was assured that they hadn't found any rats under the tarpaulin, beclogged or otherwise. I wanted to believe them, but what about the rat Peter reckoned he'd seen in Enkhuizen? He lied about the clogs; had he lied about the rat?

By the next visit, a large part of the steel roof was in place. Not the flat, two level roof I had told Anna I thought I wanted. He had said: 'You could do that, but . . ..' We listened to the 'but' bit and the advice that followed, which was that, as we had bought a nicely shaped Dutch barge, it would be nice if the roof followed the curve of the deck.

He was right of course, and we were to hear: 'You could do that, but . . ..' a few more times before we left Holland.

Back again, and we had a nearly completed, two way curved steel roof that faithfully followed the line of the deck. A fire, started whilst a doorway was being cut from the forepeak into the main hold, had solved the problem of what to do with all the rubbish in the hold. What hadn't burned, had been cleared out in case it did burn next time! We could now clearly see the floor space that would, one day, become living accommodation.

Life was becoming hectic. Backwards and forwards to

Belgium got backwards and forwards to Leeuwarden tucked into my travel itinerary, and I spent hours on P & O Ferries, drawing plans of kitchens, bedrooms and toilets. For Peter, backwards and forwards to Leeuwarden was slotted in between cobbling together avionics systems on thirty year old aircraft. In between all that, I got locked in the hotel.

The hotel is usually quite noisy. In fact, it had been ridiculously so at about five thirty that morning when I was woken by doors slamming, shrill shouts and heavy footsteps crashing on stairs.

When I left our top floor room mid-morning, I did wonder at the peaceful stillness as I made my way downstairs. On reaching the front door, I turned the handle. The door remained closed. I tried the handle again, I shook the handle and leaned against the door. It didn't yield.

A vague feeling of disquiet assailed me. I called. I called louder. Nothing and no one stirred. It was like everyone died or something. Remembering the early morning disturbance, I crept back up to our room.

Was it possible that there had been a massacre at dawn and I was the only person still alive in this bizarre place?

To reassure myself, I looked out of the window and down to the town square. A group of denim and leather teenage lads stood around the frites van with bikes and mopeds. As I watched, one of the youths collected empty frites cartons and coke and beer cans from the others, walked across the square and carefully placed the rubbish in a bin.

This wasn't real; couldn't be normal – teenagers don't behave that way! But at least there was life outside, even if it was time warped from a different era.

A noise that sounded like a vacuum cleaner encouraged me to leave my safe haven. Peering over the banister, I sighted teeth flashing in a grin from the gloom of the landing below. With relief, I saw Theodore, whole and alive, wielding a Hoover. The sound of rapidly delivered French floated up, drowning the noise of the vacuum cleaner. Cautiously making my way down to the front hall, I found Madame, looking and sounding as usual, her ever active arms gesticulating visual emphasise for some one on the other end of the telephone. Dodging low flying elbows, I made for the street door. It opened instantly to my touch.

Had I flipped? Was I cracking up from exhaustion induced by rushing around three different countries? Surely I had imagined the last twenty minutes!

Just then, I would have believed anyone who told me rats wore clogs.

'Where do you want the windows cut?' we were asked when, bearing a case of Aldi wine and a rubber plant, we made our next inspection visit to the ship yard. I produced a drawing of ten rectangular windows in measured positions.

'You could do that, but . . ..'

Here go the hands, following an imaginary curve. When a Dutch man talks about boats, his hands involuntarily produce a banana in the air. Peter is convinced that a Dutch boat builder cannot bring himself to construct straight lines. You imagine a young apprentice sneakily using a ruler to mark a line on a piece of wood. After a sleepless night, he would feel compelled to confess, and would undoubtedly be told to go and stand in the corner and recite the Dutch Boat Builders' Creed five times:

Thou shalt not covet a ruler or succumb to temptation to deliver a straight line.

We are told: 'You have allowed us to build a beautiful curved roof on a traditionally shaped barge; it would be nice if you had traditional Dutch windows.'

In Dutch, 'You have allowed us to . . .' means: 'You have agreed to pay a bit extra for.' Mind you, we were not complaining. The curved roof was very pleasing to the eye, and the extra cost not that displeasing to the pocket.

On our next trip to Leeuwarden, we could see that they were right about the ten windows with a nicely curved top. These ten curves did not actually mean any extra cost to us, but they did mean happiness to the guy who cut them.

All this sounds as if we allowed these Dutch guys to overrule our ideas and influence us to accept theirs. What actually happened was, we allowed these Dutch guys to overrule our ideas and influence us to accept theirs. We only had to look at other barges in their hands to know that these people knew their stuff. What we knew about barges didn't amount to much more than what Peter knew about knit one, purl one.

We concentrated on making the aft quarters into a cosy campsite. We now had a bed, somewhere to hang clothes, something to sit on, something to eat off, a motley collection of crockery and a rubber plant. A floor to ceiling cupboard was prepared for the installation of a shower for smallish people.

We already had a toilet. A rather remarkable toilet, with a wooden seat of a size that suggested large buttocked bargees. Beneath the seat was a heavy ceramic bowl with an eight inch aperture that led straight down to the canal. The level of canal water fluctuated with gurgles and slurps, and could be seen to rise and fall within the toilet outlet pipe. The act of flushing involved canal water being tipped down the aperture from a galvanized bucket which stood on a raised dais beside the trunk of the toilet.

The most remarkable feature of this marvel of sanitation was that it was positioned half way between the floor and the ceiling. Access was gained by, first taking a foothold on the raised dais, another one on a little blue wooden stool, then climbing up from there. Once perched on the wooden seat, a person's head needed to be tilted sideways, with one ear on the ceiling, whilst feet dangled inches above the little blue mounting stool . In the case of anyone with a less than bargee sized bum, it was necessary to grip the edge of the seat and perfect a precise balance to avoid falling into the bowl.

I discovered that, from this elevated position, it was impossible to hook the toilet roll up off the floor with a toe. Calling Peter to pass me the elusive tissue, I wailed, 'Why does it have to be so high?'

So that when the barge was loaded with cargo, the toilet bowl wouldn't be below water level and flood the crew quarters, was explained to me.

'Thank you, Peter. Would you pass the tissue now? My wrists are aching.'

Climbing down, I pointed out that we didn't intend to carry heavy cargo.

'Yes, I know,' replied Peter, 'I'll reduce the height of the toilet. I'm fed up with getting a crick in my neck every time I have a pee.'

It hadn't occurred to me that he needed to stand on the little blue stool to perform this function. He explained that, with his head pushed to a painful angle by the pressure of the ceiling, visibility became impaired and aim erratic. He had experimented with a knees bent stance, but this had jeopardised his tenuous toe curled grip on the little blue stool.

Over a half bottle of Cotes du Rhone, it was agreed that, if we were not to become deformed, constipated neurotics, the lowering of the toilet should take priority over the installation of the shower.

Neither of these tasks were accomplished by the time that, like all good things have a cliché habit of doing, the Belgian contract came to an end.

Reluctantly, we paid the last Zaventem Hotel bill, telling Theodore and Madame that, no, we would not be returning soon. If we had known at the outset that "two, maybe three weeks" meant several months, we would have shipped the parrots over and rented an apartment. But then, not only would P & O Ferries' profits have been down, but we would have missed out on the magic that is Hotel X.

After a farewell drink in the bar across the square, we bought a huge pile of mayonnaise adorned frites and drove to Leeuwarden; needing to spend a few days with Colibri. I bunged the rubber plant in a bucket of water and sponged metal grinding dust from its leaves. I was reluctant to give it to someone for safe keeping just yet; we may still have the chance to come back one more time before we called Anna and asked him to take Colibri to Enkhuizen for storage.

Back in England, we awaited the telephone call that would tell us where Peter was to be posted.

Malcom 'phoned.

A cork was pulled from a French bottle saved for a special occasion. Raising my glass, I said, 'I told you, Peter, something is directing us!'

'And I told you, Meg, it's all Malcom's fault!'

Clinking glasses, we drank to Peter's new overseas contract.

Where?

Belgium!

Chapter Four

TAKING BABY HOME

We could have refused on the basis that it wasn't far over many seas, or even that the sun doesn't shine that often. Well, it does in summer, but this was winter!

Peter could have said an emphatic 'No, Malcom!'

Peter said, 'Thank you, Malcom, that's great!'

'Super,' said Malcom. 'We'd like you to report back to Brussels Airport at the beginning of January.'

The sensible thing to do was to book a room in the Zaventem Hotel for January and spend December in our warm comfortable home in England. What we did was stuff household effects, warm clothing, an assortment of tools and two parrots into the jeep and headed for Colibri's aft crew quarters.

The transforming of fun weekend camping accommodation into *of course we can live in here in winter* accommodation couldn't possibly involve anything worse than hard work, discomfort and major privation.

Friesland is damn cold in December! Quite likely, not many people beyond Frieslanders and a few thousand cows know that. Any other well balanced person would have no reason to be there in December to discover the true meaning of the 'Fries' in Friesland.

To be fair, Leeuwarden is an interesting Northern Dutch town. The canal winds it's way through, and the town boasts a beautiful church that leans at an angle not unlike that of the Tower of Pisa. Traffic is brought to a halt when a herd of live cows want to cross the road and, not unexpectedly, a large stone statue of a cow dominates the town square. It is probably significant that the female gender was cast in stone; given that even a hardy native would be unwilling to expose the male's biological parts to these temperatures.

There was no running plumbing in Colibri's aft crew quarters. Let's face it, there was no normally considered normal convenience or facility anywhere in Colibri. I had to collect water in plastic wine tubs from the shipyard's work barge on a daily basis. Somebody considered this to come under the heading of housekeeping, therefore, Meg's department.

Peter's priority was to coax a smelly little diesel heater into some sort of performance approaching a heat giving one. The parrots, doing a penguin act, huddled together in a corner of their makeshift cage, and the one called Dillon said 'Bonjour' whenever she heard Dutch voices. Having picked the word up when we took Tiger Lily through France, she now applies it to any non English speakers.

Of course, the Dutch do speak English. Most of the ones we met did anyway; usually pretty good English. A ship yard welder would speak to us in Dutch, and we would ask, 'Do you speak English?' If you watched the eyes very carefully, you could almost see a floppy disk being changed in the two second delay before the response, 'A little,' came through - followed by fluent, articulate English!

Dillon taught the welders to say 'Oh shit!' An expression she picked up from me when the diesel heater went out. This more or less daily occurrence was preceded by a black puff of foul smelling smoke, a minor bang and a highly explosive Oh Shit!

Peee- ter! in a shrill voice, was another thing Dillon picked up at that time, along with a cute little expletive, that I'm reluctant to commit to print, which we blamed on the Dutch welders.

The shipyard's work was finished. Colibri was ready to be discharged from the tender care of those who had nursed her thus far. With concern for her future development, the shipyard boss discussed our conversion plans with us. The materials we needed were cheaper here than in Belgium he told us, and he would be happy to order them from his own suppliers.

'Good job we're designed to carry cargo,' I commented as, day by day, shipyard workers cheerfully loaded giant rolls of insulation, endless packs of pine ceiling board, marine plywood and timber into the hold until the place began to resemble a B & Q clearance sale.

I heard Peter discussing a delivery of cement with someone in the wheelhouse. An English, West Country voice was offering the use of the yard's crane. Intrigued, I peered up from the aft quarters. A blonde haired, round faced, very Dutch looking guy grinned down at me.

'Hi, I'm Derrik,' said the Pam Ayres accent.

'But, surely, you're Dutch?'

'I am indeed.'

'But, you speak English with a West Country accent!'

'Sorry about that; I spent a year in Dorset.'

A Year! What is it with these Dutch? Are they born with an integral language programme or what? Or is it that they have to speak other languages because no one else speaks Dutch? I mean, it is reasonable to suppose that, if you were a Dutch man in Dorset, you would have to learn to speak English rather speedily in order to communicate at all.

Whatever, I didn't have much time to ponder this; it was the man's body I was interested in just then. Being big and burly, Derrik of the Dorset drawl was one of our main assets in the attempt to sink Colibri with tax free materials.

Hydrophores are expensive, we are told.

'What the hell's a hydrosphere?' I ask.

'A water pressure pump,' I am told. I am also told the price.

'Do we really need one of those hydra things?' I ask.

'Do you really want hot and cold water running out of taps and showers?' Peter asks.

We bought a hydrophore.

By means of a rather amazing feat of engineering that called for an assortment of metric and obsolete imperial fittings, Peter plumbed together five of the stainless steel water tanks we had inherited with the barge. With one connection left to go – the vital one that would eventually marry the tanks to the miracle of science called a hydrophore – he ran out of fittings. Not the sort that you can just nip round to the local D.I.Y. shop and buy, but the difficult to obtain sort that went out with World War Two.

Faced with the task of having to redo the whole intricate network of master plumbing, Peter took a coffee break, just as a peculiar looking object – which I was told was called a hydrophore – arrived on the fraught scene. The bearer of this equipment knew exactly where to obtain a World War Two plumbing relic.

Without much optimism, Peter proffered a sixty year old piece of copper and iron pipe to a man behind a Dickensian style counter and asked if there was any chance of a fitting that would, sort of, fit. The shop assistant changed floppy disks and said, 'Come with me, you can search for what you need.' He and Peter disappeared down some steps and I sat down to wait.

I watched, fascinated, as a customer entered the shop and, finding no one to serve him, measured a length of rope from a large drum, went behind the counter and found some scissors, cut the rope, scribbled on a scrap of paper, left a pile of coins on top of the till, said, 'Good day,' to me and left the shop.

How did he know to speak to me in English? Was the rumour out in Leeuwarden that we were in town, or was it my amazed, jaw hanging expression that gave me away?

The shop assistant returned without Peter. Peter re-appeared twenty minutes or so later clutching a handful of pipe fittings. 'You should see that cellar!' he told me. 'It's like Alladin's cave. Full of everything imaginable from every conceivable era!'

After gleefully dumping his treasures on my lap, Peter asked for thirty metres of electrical wire. The assistant tucked a drum of wire under his arm and went out through the street door. With a shrug, Peter followed him then popped his head round the door to tell me to come and help.

The shop assistant was kneeling on the ground holding the end of the wire on a painted line on the pavement. I was told to carry the drum to a parking meter, round it and back to the painted line. Uncoiling wire as I went, I circumnavigated the parking meter, vaguely wondering why I was doing this, and wondering at the indifference of pedestrians and dogs who stepped over my wire and walked round me, ignoring me as if I was behaving perfectly normally.

Obviously satisfied that we knew what we were doing, the assistant left us to it and returned to his other customers. Once I had returned the drum of wire to Peter, he placed it on the painted line on the pavement and cut it.

'You see,' said Peter – now an authority on these things – 'from here to the parking meter is fifteen metres. So, there and back again is the thirty metres we want.'

Simple really.

By the time we were all stocked up and nervously thinking of leaving the safe haven of the ship yard, we had learned to call our barge a ship. In Holland, Colibri was a scheep and we were scheepers. In Holland, Colibri was a very small ship. What we had gazed up at in awe and called a helluva lot of boat was a little over half the length of the smaller barges in Holland and Belgium. Later, in small canals in France, Colibri would become a big peniche, but here, her eighty seven feet made her very small fry. Nevertheless, she was a monster vessel to us.

We had both helmed a hundred and twelve foot brigantine in the open spaces of the South China Sea, but driving eighty seven feet of barge in busy European waterways, where huge commercial ships move at high speed, was a daunting prospect. It was mid December, with few daylight hours and the likely handicap of fog. We asked at the shipyard if there was a local barge skipper we could engage to accompany us to Brussels.

Johan was brought to meet us. Johan was a young, fresh faced, energetic, enthusiastic and experienced skipper. He suggested that we allow four days for the journey and suggested a price for his services.

Johan was not expensive and he proved to be worth every Guilder. His cheerfulness and sense of humour alone were good value, apart from his confidence and skill.

Sleeping accommodation was a problem we thought. Johan thought not. He was very happy with our little two man tent erected in the cargo hold. Six inch nails banged into the floor held guyropes and the many rolls of insulation, positioned round the tent, served to offer protection from the iciness of the unheated hold. Being envious of anyone who didn't have to sleep with the dubious benefit of our mean little diesel heater, I was tempted to change places, but Peter refused to swap sleeping partners.

What about the jeep? I suddenly wondered. How would we get that and a barge to Brussels? Meg could drive the jeep, leaving Johan and Peter to drive the barge, was suggested. But Meg didn't want to drive the jeep. Meg wanted to be firmly on board for her baby's first steps.

The jeep would go on Colibri's roof, was another suggestion. It would, easily, but being a high vehicle, it would obscure vision from the wheel house. Whoever was driving, wouldn't be able to see over it.

'It can be done,' said Johan, 'But if we have fog or something . . .'

We opted for vision. We didn't need difficulty programmed into this expedition.

Time to shake hands and say goodbye to people who had been in our lives for some months and had played an important role in act one of the Colibri saga.

'See you next year,' said the Pam Ayres soundalike.

'Why?' we asked.

He explained that lots of people take on an empty barge with the intention of converting it themselves, but they all come back to either have it converted or buy one already completed.

'Watch this space,' we told him. 'You'll see a first.'

'Sure,' he said. 'See you next year.'

Colibri didn't look a picture of refined elegance when we left Leeuwarden. Her hull and bollards would have to receive paint in the spring and the new steel roof, we were advised, must be left to rust for six months before paint was applied. There were burn streaks along the side coaming where the windows had been cut out and, in all honesty, Colibri looked like a rusty heap; a tramp ship that we were, nevertheless, very proud of.

With green and red navigation lights glowing eerily in the misty dark, we set out at six thirty a.m. As I understood it, our first obstacle was a lifting bridge. It would lift – briefly – at seven a.m. and we must be in position and ready to pass through.

As it happened, the first obstacle was persuading solidly frozen ropes to relinquish their hold on our mooring bollards. You can't casually flip a stiff loop from an object it is ice welded to. Neither can you easily coil a frozen length of rope. Having managed to prise the loop from the metal shore bollard, I found it wasn't a case of simply pulling it on board. The loop remained a frozen 'O' on a rigid stem, looking like an empty lollipop on a pole. Or a giant version of Miss Rosalind's Romper Room mirror. I heard Peter say, 'And I can see you.' I couldn't see him from my position on the foredeck, but I knew he was peering through a similar frozen loop at the stern.

Johan was at the wheel, easing Colibri from the quay. Several tons of ice being displaced by several tons of boat produced the weirdest sounds I have ever heard. A series of sharp explosions mingled with long, drawn out, high pitched sighs echoed across the canal as the breaks we created spread far out and into cracks around and before us. Fragments of ice, like shattered panes of frosted glass, swirled in our wake.

Feeling that I well and truly qualified for The Crypton Factor, I cautiously shuffled down the length of the glazed side deck; not daring to retain a hold on the roof for more than a few seconds at a time in case my gloves became welded to the steel. I was not pleased to see Peter and Johan laughing at me as I neared the safety of the wheelhouse. But I suppose if I was witnessing a shape, barely discernible as human in it's bulging layer of clothes, emulating a lunar walk in slow motion at six thirty on a misty morning, I would have been amused too. As it was, I was gravely concentrating on solving the problem of where to search for my thermal vests – if I ever reached the aft quarters in safety.

I forgot all about my vests in the excitement of watching a bridge hinge up from the canal bank. Not to mention the anxiety of watching that it stayed suspended above until we had fully passed beneath.

With most of the time spent with my head under the bed searching for clothes bags likely to yield a thermal vest or two, the first stretch of the Van Harinxma Canal was unobserved by me. It was still dark outside anyway. Mid morning, we passed through a lock at Harlingen and we were suddenly at sea. Colibri was tossed about for an hour and a half before she was turned into another lock and out the other end into the Ijsselmeer.

We were well used to driving the road alongside this land locked sea, and we had seen it look rough and angry, even in summer. Being an easy victim to sea sickness, I was not looking forward to this bit. We had been warned that bow waves over the foredeck could be serious, so had nailed a thick sheet of plywood over the newly cut front entrance to the cargo hold. Just to be sure, thick floorboards were then nailed across to hold the ply firmly in place.

The Ijsselmeer was a docile lake that cold, clear day in mid December. We glided through calm water like a plastic dinghy in a swimming pool. This was an unexpected bonus; there had been some trepidation about taking an unknown boat into these often hazardous waters. For most of the twenty six miles to the next lock at Enkhuizen, we were out of sight of land, with a compass that we dare not rely on because of it being surrounded by new metal.

I wasn't told about that bit when the wheel was offered. This was my first chance to helm our new vessel and I grabbed it and the wheel whilst Peter and Johan attempted to sweep the decks free of several month's worth of metal *grin-ding* dust. Had we been in sight of land or another ship, alarm may have been raised by the spectacle of a somewhat dilapidated barge travelling at high speed under an orange pall.

The Markermeer inland sea that followed was equally kind. Making eleven knots, Johan was optimistic that we would reach Amsterdam before dark. A little too optimistic. Night began to descend as we approached Amsterdam Harbour a little after four o'clock. We had a lock to pass through before entering the harbour, and I was enchanted to see a large fir tree festooned with fairy lights on the lockside.

Johan's back was visible from the wheelhouse as he stood on the side deck apparently gazing at the festive tree. I picked up the camera and set the flash. A picture of our trusty Dutch skipper, with the tree in the background, would make a lovely memento of this trip.

Creeping carefully down the icy deck to get Johan at a better angle, I pointed the camera, pressed the button and took a flashlit photograph of a brightly lit Christmas tree and our trusty skipper having a pee over the side.

Once we got into the harbour, the plan was to moor for the night. This involved me; I was going to have to go outside and do things with ropes. I reckoned I had time for a quick pee before donning a few more layers of clothing. If only I knew where my thermal vests were!

I climbed onto the loo and balanced myself. A difficult feat with a pair of woollen tights, jeans and leg warmers round my ankles, some of which needed to be hitched up to knee height to leave feet free to step onto the raised dais then the little blue stool. Once enthroned, I relinquished my hold on the bundle of leg wear because I needed both hands to clutch the seat.

Some 'quick pee' this!

There was a sudden roar of engine, my world shuddered violently and I increased the intensity of my grip on the big wooden seat. As a surge of canal water shot up the toilet aperture and engulfed my bottom, I promptly lost my grip and fell into the toilet bowl. An urge to leap up in panic was thwarted by the fact that the subsequent down rush of water created a vacuum in which my buttocks became firmly held. All I could do was sit with knees in the air, thinking: 'Oh hell! This is Amsterdam Harbour – the water is filthy! I'll get dysentery, or hepatitis, or verrucas or something – or everything!'

In that moment of stress I learned the meaning of the term "positive thinking". Thoughts of verrucas and/or everything imaginable were positive enough to propel me into taking advantage of the next upsurge of contaminated water and haul myself up onto the toilet seat. Gasping from the icy impact, I reached a foot down towards the little blue stool. My foot made contact with space. Peering down, I saw that the stool had toppled off the dais and was now wedged between the dais and the door, making it impossible to open from inside or out. This called for more positive thinking and a considerable amount of twisting, groping and grunting. The limited space didn't allow for bending to obtain full arm employment, and my legs were inhibited by being encased in several layers of concertinaed clothing. I was left with no choice but to close my eyes and launch myself onto the dais. With one set of outstretched fingers and one set of upturned toes, I eventually managed to dislodge the obstructing stool before throwing open the loo door with a dramatic gesture and an outraged bellow:

'Thanks, Guys. I just had an ultra chilled enema!'

What did I expect? Sympathy, concern, apologies even? What I got was Johan's face grinning down at my dishevelled semi dressed figure and his droll comment, 'So, you are lucky, this ship has a bidet.'

When they managed to stop laughing, Peter and Johan explained that a ship had suddenly appeared out of the dark across our bow, causing them to throw Colibri into sudden and violent full reverse. An excuse that I didn't feel justified the state they threw me into!

I wasn't allowed time to grizzle – or even finish dressing – because mooring alongside several other barges took everyone's attention. I plopped a rope onto deck bollards of a barge that was so derelict I hoped the weight of our rope wouldn't sink it, taking us down with it into the murky depths as we slept. The aroma emanating from the haze that hung in the still air suggested that we had chosen one of Amsterdam's many junkie ships as an overnight neighbour. Maybe it was the influence of this atmosphere or just sheer fatigue that made us all sleep like logs.

Taking advantage of first light, ropes were off early next morning. Ten minutes later, we were squinting through thick fog, trying to see somewhere to moor up again. We could hear ships moving around us, but we couldn't see any of them. It was after nine before visibility improved sufficiently for safe exit from Amsterdam Harbour. But, how the hell to get out? We didn't even know exactly where we were! Amsterdam Harbour is an enormous complex – worse than the car parks at Heathrow – and some skilful turns and direction guessing brought us, eventually, into the stretch of canal we needed to take us on to Utrecht.

All we had to cope with then was snow. I dived below and wrote some Christmas cards, kicking the diesel heater as I passed; daring it to go out. I didn't actually achieve very many Christmas greetings because I kept being distracted by the white Christmassy scene floating by the window. When Peter called down that we were approaching a lock, I decided against risking the loo before piling on some woolly layers for the sortie down the snow clad side deck.

I stood on the foredeck, clutching a rope and debating whether there was any point in asking again – but calmly this time – where Peter had hidden the blue canvas bag that my thermal vests were packed in. It was as I dismissed this idea that another question began to form in my partially frozen brain. It began with: 'Why?' I pushed what I already suspected was going to be a negative thought aside and concentrated, instead, on not letting Colibri slide into the barge in front.

The partially born thought hovered, became insidious; determined to become fully born. Whilst thirty three point three per cent of my mind concentrated on my rope and thirty three point three per cent on the space between us and the barge in front, the remaining thirty three point three per cent allowed the submerged thought to surface, kicking and screaming. It went something like: 'Why the . . . are we doing this?'

The locking completed, I groped my way back to the wheelhouse. Warmth emanated from the little camping gas heater and from Johan in a mere three layers. Under an anorak hood and balaclava, I flexed stiff lips. Peering from beneath layers of showerproof nylon, polyester lining and knitting wool, I announced, 'Last year, I was sailing the Med. in a bikini. The year before, I was swimming in the Arabian Gulf. Three years ago, I ate barbecued Christmas turkey on a Borneo beach. We have a warm, comfortable home in England. Can some one please tell me why the . . . we are doing this?'

'Because,' replied Peter, 'there are three sides to a coin.'

He also said he would do the rest of the locks on his own – cheeky sod, there weren't anymore before Dordrecht.

The crew of another barge that passed from behind was having to cope with snow without the benefit of a wheelhouse. We waved and gestured sympathy. Further on we passed the same barge and again exchanged waves.

Was this shades of the A12 and a grey Ford Fiesta? Yep, later the barge overtook us again. From their open bridge the crew pointed stiff fingers at our wheelhouse and gestured envy. We came across the other barge again at a junction. A choice of three directions was on offer here, and the other barge was hovering, uncertainly, mid canal. The crew's brains must have been in cold storage by then, and we believe that they were totally disorientated in the swirling snow. Looking back, we saw them turn into a branch off the main canal.

'They've blown it,' said Johan. 'They shouldn't have gone that way.'

Thoughts of two frozen men, open to the elements and trying to get unlost, at least made me appreciate our rotten little diesel heater. Okay, so we missed our own turning, but as it was getting dark anyway, it seemed prudent to moor in a little harbour that presented itself beyond where we were supposed to have gone.

This left us with the task, next day, of backing out of the little harbour into the busy main waterway of the Oude Maas. The M25 had nothing on this, and we still had to cross the flow of traffic and the fast flow of current in order to go back to where we should have turned off into the Dordtse Canal the previous night.

Travelling down the Hollands Diep with a rapid current and

huge, high speed sea going ships, with the added excitement of fog, is an episode that shouldn't be dwelt on. So I won't dwell. It actually means more to me that we arrived at the Belgian border that night.

We were nearly home, but first, it was necessary to go through the act of exporting Colibri from Holland. The only mooring we could see when we stopped on the Belgian side of the border, was a row of posts in the water; obviously placed for ships somewhat larger than Colibri. So it was that, in the morning, when Johan and Peter walked back to Holland to the border lock with a file of paperwork, I was left on board a ship that was suspended between two posts. I stood in the wheelhouse and estimated the chances of one of our ropes letting us down. I had visions of the two guys returning to find Colibri swinging mid stream from one rope, and an hysterical woman wondering how on earth she was going to get the ship to land so the skipper could get back on board! It was only then that I realized I didn't even know how to start the engine.

We had thought that driving through Antwerp by car was something to be experienced. Antwerp by boat made the A12, M25 and Brentwood High Street combined fade into insignificance.

We arrived at the lock in good time, and the weather was behaving itself reasonably. At midday, Peter reported to lock control for permission to go through into the tidal River Schelde. We were ship number fourteen for the next locking.

'At 14.30,' we were told, 'you will follow ship number thirteen into the lock.'

By 14.15, the wind had decided to join in the action. Even Johan's expertise was stretched by the complexities of guiding a light weight, cargoless barge amongst other ships all with 14.30 appointments.

By 15.00, all seventeen ships were in position and the lock gates closed. Both gates, at both ends, stayed closed. Bargee wives went shopping; others cleaned already pristine wheelhouse windows and some fetched frites from somewhere. Johan wondered if he had time to go and 'phone his wife, but was reluctant to leave in case there was a sudden exodus from the lock. Over the next two hours, no boats moved. What were we waiting for?

For the tide to turn, would you believe? The water outside the lock was higher than the water inside the lock, making it impossible to open the gates and let us all out.

After two hours, the tide turned and the River Schelde dropped to the level inside the lock. By the time the gates opened and seventeen ships surged forward, night had descended in inky blackness. Because we couldn't see anywhere to moor immediately outside the lock, we drove into the darkness. Unsure what to do next, we headed towards a lighted area and found a wharf with a large restaurant ship attached to it. Diving in front of the restaurant ship, we grabbed at some land bollards that were fast disappearing above our heads. With one bollard being way forward of us, and one well behind, we hoped we would be able to hold steady.

The water was dropping at an alarming rate, and Colibri was soon far below land. We couldn't get ashore; we were marooned. Johan called on the ship's radio to ask how low the water was expected to fall. Between six and seven metres was the news. News that was followed by three people frantically tying together all ropes on board. Our initial mooring ropes were already stretched to their limit.

By the time we had dropped eight metres, Peter and Johan were placing bets on which of our ropes would snap first. None snapped, but Colibri was beginning to tilt sideways before the water became slack. Satisfied that we had stopped dropping, the two men went to bed to try and grab some sleep.

Wide awake, nursing anxiety, I was the first to become aware that the tide had turned. From slack water, an inrush of tide brought high winds with it for company. All hell broke loose, mainly in the form of Meg yelling at two exhausted men. Colibri was smashing against the wall, and I was convinced that we would all end up as so much flotsam floating up with the vicious waves. I didn't get the chance to go totally to pieces; it was a case of all hands on deck to wind in the slackening ropes as we rode up the wall. When Colibri's wheelhouse roof was Johan's height from land, he hauled himself up to go and 'phone his wife. I wonder if she appreciated a call at four thirty a.m.

Ten hours after we left it we returned to ground level and, with relief, stepped ashore. I thought we had left vulnerability behind when we abandoned our ocean sailing plans! The most valuable lesson any boat traveller can learn is to respect the elements. Man will never conquer, or even be equal to, wind and water – even if he does think he controls motorways.

The Brussels Canal was half a day away. Johan's time with us was officially up, but he had 'phoned his wife to say he would stay long enough to escort us into calm water. Everybody was happy when we took Colibri through the Lock at Wintam and into non-tidal water. Leaving the lock and the rumbustious River Schelde behind, Peter pointed to some heavy wooden mooring posts.

'Not good to tie to those,' said Johan, 'A big ship may come and lean against you.'

We felt we had had enough excitement for a while, and Johan reckoned we would be safe behind the mooring posts. So, with practised skill, Johan tucked Colibri out of harm's way between the posts and the bank. A rusty iron stake protruded from the bank, as did a disused fence post. We put three ropes onto these and had lunch with a good helping of red wine.

When Johan's wife came to collect what was left of him, we suggested that he may need to be pampered for a few days.

'Well, we're on our own now,' said Peter, waving to the boot of Johan's car.

We crashed into bed and slept till evening.

Next day, with the excuse that it would do us good to walk on land, we trekked to a nearby village and bought food. After lunch, we said it would do us good to have a rest. In truth, we were putting off the time when we would have to move our barge on our own. We would do it tomorrow.

Morning fog ruled out an early start, but we couldn't keep procrastinating; we had to move this thing sometime!

'Right, let's go for it,' said Peter when he could see the other side of the wide canal. He took one of the three ropes off. I took a second one off, then put my hand on the final one and looked down the length of the boat at Peter. Standing at the wheel, engine running, he nodded. I undid the rope from the ship's bollard. Holding onto the rope, I looked ashore to where the other end was still round a fence post. We were still attached to land; it wasn't too late to chicken out.

'Take it off,' called Peter from the wheelhouse. I pulled the last rope on board, and we and Colibri were adrift, all by ourselves, for the first time!

Shoulders hunched with tension, Peter manoeuvred his barge out from behind the mooring posts. With a slight lowering of Peter's shoulders, we moved along the canal. A barge came towards us. We passed it and went through a bridge.

'I think we can do this,' said Peter, his shoulders reverting to their normal position.

All went well until we came to a bridge that looked rather low. We couldn't be sure that we could get under it. Actually, that went well as it happens. A barge passed from behind and, as it drew alongside, we judged it to be higher than Colibri. So, when it passed happily under the bridge, we followed. Then things didn't go quite so well.

The next bridge was very definitely too low. It was at street level, and cars drove across it. We leaned against the bank and waited for the man in the glass control box to stop the traffic and lift the bridge. Two more ships arrived and waited. The traffic drove across the bridge in a constant stream and the man in the glass control box ate some sandwiches.

Aware that we could be here for ages, and thinking that the practice would be useful, we moved across the canal and put some ropes round a crash barrier. More ships arrived and the crash barrier became congested. After lunch, three men turned up with tool boxes. An hour later, the bridge's mechanism was restored to working order, the road traffic came to a halt and six ships fired up engines and moved forward. The seventh ship - guess who - waited until the congestion had cleared before following. The barge we followed cleared the bridge then stopped suddenly to pick up a woman with shopping bags. Peter learned, quite quickly, how to pull round a stationary object and avoid being guillotined by a lowering bridge.

We still had to tackle a lock on our own. Before we reached it, other ships steamed up from behind and overtook us. The lifting bridge was obviously still lifting.

In pouring rain and impending darkness, the huge Zemst lock loomed. All the other ships had been swallowed up by the lock and, dubious about jostling with them for space, we wondered about mooring up for the night and negotiating the lock in daylight.

It was so murky, we couldn't see anywhere to moor. At ground level, the lock was a blaze of lights. This made it difficult to see, at water level, exactly where the entrance was. We dithered, unsure what to do.

'We're going for the lock,' announced Peter.

'But, how do we know we can get in?' I wanted to know.

'If that damn great tanker can get in, I reckon we can.'

'What damn great tanker?'

'The one that's just about to overtake us.'

Personally, I thought the term "Damn great tanker" was a gross understatement. If there had been any sunlight, the ship would have completely blotted it out as it passed. At least it showed us where to go and, more by luck than judgement, we entered the lock in it's wake as the vast gate was beginning to close.

A man on the lockside, way above my head, shouted and gesticulated wildly. I have no idea what he was on about. Maybe we shouldn't have come in; it's possible that we should have announced ourselves on the radio. We must have taken the man by surprise, suddenly appearing out of the gloom and bobbing around in his highly organized lock like a recalcitrant bath toy.

I could see just one unoccupied floating bollard set in the lock wall just above the water surface. I pointed and Peter headed for it. Closer inspection showed that, instead of a floating bollard, this one was a fifty per cent sinking bollard. I had to act quickly! From about ten feet, I threw a rope. One of my better throws actually; the rope landed directly above the bollard – which, by now, had become a hundred per cent sunk. My rope settled on the water, then floated back towards me.

We were adrift in an eight hundred by eighty foot lock which had already started its huge rise to ground level!

Hearing a voice call "Colibri", I turned to see a man indicating that we should go alongside his damn great tanker. My throw at the sinking bollard had been a demonstration of practised and efficient rope handling. My throw at the man's outstretched hand was a diabolical cock-up. The fact that I was standing on the rope was contributory to the fact that the loop landed in the water, several yards short of one outstretched hand. I was a bundle of nerves and my retrieved rope was a bundle of tangles. Something about the man's unhurried, completely calm instructions to try again, enabled me to coil the rope and succeed in delivering it into capable hands, just as our bow threatened to make severe contact with this nice shipper's immaculate paintwork. Mr. Nice brushed aside my thanks and my apologies for splattering him with wet rope and secured Colibri to a bollard on his deck. At least we knew this one would float up with us.

The far gate opened and a flotilla of hefty ships and barges surged forward. Colibri must have looked like a small child taking part in an adult activity. It was dark out there; it would have been ever so nice to leave the umbilical cord attached to our kindly grown up ship and just go with it – wherever.

Trailing out behind the burly fleet, we sighted lights over to our right. Straining to see through stinging sleet, we glimpsed what looked like a long wall and a row of bollards. It beckoned invitingly, and we headed for it, hoping it wasn't a mirage.

It was indeed a long wall. A very long, very solid wall, with lots of monster bollards that, from a bulbous top, tapered down to a waist bigger than mine.

Our first solo voyage with Colibri was over and we were safely nestled against a sturdy wall. Over a hot meal, tension seeped out. With the last dregs of a wine bottle, exhaustion crept in. Not bothering to undress, we collapsed into bed; convinced that we would sleep for a week.

Chapter Five

TEETHING PROBLEMS

At first light, we were wakened by a bright frosty day glaring through uncurtained widows. Like a couple of excited kids, we scrambled out of a tangle of sleeping bags to go and see where we were.

Daylight revealed a very pleasant scene. The canal was wide here; stretching some two hundred yards across to the far bank. Beside us were trees and fields. A narrow, surfaced road led to the mooring wall then petered out into a little leafy lane.

A barge that, like Colibri, looked as if it was thinking of becoming a converted barge, was moored at the far end of the long wall. It had the air of a boat that hadn't moved for a long time. This suggested that, maybe, we could leave Colibri here whilst we went back to fetch the jeep.

But where was Here? We'd need to know where to drive back to. Walking along the narrow road, we came to a sign telling us the name of the village. We looked at each other and said, 'Where!'

The sign said: Kappelle Op den Bos.

A difficult decision had to be made before we left the barge to go to Leeuwarden. Should we leave the diesel heater off and risk the parrots expiring from exposure, or should we leave it alight and risk the parrots being asphyxiated by black smoke and fumes? I won the toss. We left the parrots to freeze on the basis that, if the heater blew up, we would loose the boat as well as two parrots.

We walked to Kappelle Op den Bos station to get a train to Mechelin, to get a train to Amsterdam, to get a train to Leeuwarden. Standing in a downpour of sleet on a platform at Mechelin station, we wished we had been able to bring the jeep on Colibri's deck. I suggested to Peter that he should buy me a car small enough to go on board – something low slung, like a Lotus Elan, I thought.

I was asked which I would prefer, a low slung car or a low slung toilet.

After a gruelling train journey North and several hours drive back in wintery conditions, it was nearly midnight before we parked the jeep beside Colibri. There was no welcoming whistle or Hello from the birds when we went on board. With some anxiety, we entered a boat that felt even colder than the sub zero outside air.

Small wonder the birds were silent – we had covered their cage with a thick blanket in an attempt to preserve them. The poor things thought it had been night time since we left early that morning!

For two or three days, we drove around looking for a more permanent mooring. We didn't find anywhere as nice as our current one, but we didn't know if we would be allowed to stay there. The long wall was used by commercial ships, and we could well be in the way. However, it was a few days before Christmas and we thought that no one would hassle us for the time being.

At the end of December, we met the owner of the barge at the far end of the wall; a diminutive Belgian who spoke fluent English. When asked how long it was permitted to moor here, he told us that twenty four hours was allowed. We had already been there for about two hundred and forty hours, so we asked what happened after twenty four hours.

'You can stay another twenty four hours, then another twenty four hours, until some one asks you to leave,' he explained. 'Then you must go, but you can come back again for twenty four hours.'

We asked how long his boat had been there and he told us for nearly two years.

We considered taking the same sort of twenty four hour deal. It was very nice here and the nearby village had all we needed. The discovery of a small but well stocked and extremely obliging, D.I.Y. shop and timber yard clinched it. Peter bought me a really smart, expensive Sandvik saw and we settled down in our new home.

Canal traffic, which had been fairly light over the Christmas period, became heavier. After experiencing some heavy surges of water caused by passing ships, Peter put additional ropes to shore and doubled up on tyres between us and the wall before leaving me whilst he went to work. He also lowered the toilet. Some of the heavier surges moved the boat quite seriously, and I think Peter had visions of me being unseated and stuck in a loo bowl waiting for him to come home and rescue me.

Because the aircraft came in and went out at night, Peter went out at night and came in in the morning. He had to sleep in the daytime, and living in an area twelve by fifteen feet with one awake person, one sleeping person, two noisy parrots and a smelly diesel heater is not the easiest situation that I know of. I often had to put a cover over the birds' cage, saying, 'Shsh! Peter's sleeping.' This was when we discovered that Dillon has a speech impediment. She has a problem with esses, and when Storm squawked, she said, 'Shsh! Peter'sh shleeping.'

All in all, this was a rather difficult period. It was bitterly cold, and the stupid heater, that worked like a dream when Peter was home during the day, had a habit of going bang – pouf – out at night. My head got really cold when I opened a window to release the foul black smoke. I bought a rubber hot water bottle and knitted a woolly bobble hat.

It was nice when Peter came home at seven in the morning. I enjoyed the cup of tea he brought me and he enjoyed getting into a pre-warmed bed. One morning, when I thought it would be rather nice to stay snuggled in bed with Peter, a huge ship belted past and a particularly vicious surge lifted Colibri up and bounced her sideways against the tyres on the wall. The boat twitched on mooring ropes that had become giant rubber bungees and a pile of books tumbled off a shelf and showered the bed.

Releasing his grip on the mattress, Peter asked, 'Did the earth move for you too, Darling?'

I really didn't like being left on my own at night in this strange place where people spoke a funny language. Even if there were any people around, which was rare, I wouldn't know how to ask for help if I needed it. Occasionally, a nearby barge would run a generator during the day or evening, but at night, it was uncannily quiet. Unless a lock full of ships was disgorged, it was so quiet that, when I strained to hear something, anything, the silence buzzed in my ears. Me, who had become paranoid about noise, now wanted to hear at least the swish of passing car tyres, or an owl hoot.

I would have been ecstatic to hear a telephone ring. What if I needed a telephone in the night? This would necessitate a walk of at least half a mile to the nearest 'phone box at the lock. But then, why would I need a 'phone? Our rusty old tramp ship was hardly attractive to burglars and anyway, there was a distinct absence of crime around here. There wasn't even any graffiti. Telephone equipment, intact and undamaged, sitting complacently inside local 'phone boxes that boasted whole panes of glass and untorn directories, indicated a serious deficit of vandalism.

Secured by five hefty ropes to giant bollards designed to hold ships of the super tanker calibre, Colibri was unlikely to come adrift. To be honest, there was nothing to really concern me except tremendous gales and high winds.

To be honest, these really concerned me!

Standing in the wheelhouse one wind torn evening, we watched a row of trees fall like a row of dominoes across the canal side road. What happened next, we watched in further amazement. Teams of men and trucks arrived and started clearing the road whilst the storm still raged. We had assumed that the electricity cable, taken down by falling trees, would mean the lights on the mooring wall would be out for days. Not so; this was Belgium, and all was restored to order within twenty four hours. Incredible, considering that the little road, so quickly cleared, led to nowhere except the mooring wall and a little leafy lane.

There were several sessions of severely strong winds during February. The hatch in the aft quarters roof opened and closed like a giant mouth shouting: "Windy!" We screwed it down to the frame to shut it up, then discovered that particularly exuberant gusts were able to lift the entire frame. It was like a monster who, having had its mouth firmly clamped, was lifting its chin in defiance. Just to be on the safe side, we fixed a rope to the hatch and tied the other end onto the settee. Not only did we have to keep ducking under the rope, but I lived in fear of the settee being yanked off the floor and becoming embedded in the ceiling.

The diminutive Belgian had similar problems on his barge. Concerned that his partially fitted steel roof might blow away, he tied it down to a toilet in the hold. A sheet of eight by four foot steel, only tack welded in place, did blow off and into the canal – taking a toilet with it.

Although I never did need a telephone at night, I needed one when Peter was late home from work one morning. Very late, as in two hours late – and there was a gale blowing. Imagining my husband crushed in a corrugated yellow jeep under a fallen tree, I needed to 'phone the airport and hear that a gale induced disaster had befallen an aircraft and delayed Peter safely at work.

In order to put my mind at rest, I had to expose my body to flying twigs and falling branches to get to the lock 'phone box. In magazines and things, you read phrases like: "The wind took her breath away". It wasn't quite like that for me. This force eight monster forced its way up my nostrils and reached down to grab my breath before it had a chance to leave my lungs. If I looked up, it was impossible to breathe. With head down, chin on chest, it was difficult to breathe; but difficult was better than impossible and anyway, it was all I had. I wanted to take a deep breath occasionally before looking up but, this being out of the question, I made do with total suspension of breathing at intervals in order to keep an eye out for trees leaning at an angle precarious enough to make me a victim of the fate I'd got worked out for Peter.

Of course, the daytime switchboard operator had no knowledge of the whereabouts of anyone who worked at night. Not only had my risky and arduous trek to the 'phone box been futile, I was furious when I saw an uncreased yellow jeep bowling past. Blast him! He was safe, and I still had to run the gauntlet of flying debris to get home again.

With the wind up my tail and my feet only sometimes managing to act as landing gear, my return journey was like a high speed replay of my outward journey. It was made very clear to Peter that, if he ever again had technical discussions over breakfast in the airport bar during a gale, it would be a divorce job.

Leaving the parrots uncovered and telling them to squawk their hearts out, I went into the hold and attacked some pine ceiling board with a varnish brush. We do know that those particular boards will never rot for want of thoroughly worked in varnish!

In spite of all these distractions, conversion of the hold into living accommodation was well under way. Priority was to line the roof with fibreglass insulation before cladding it with the pine ceiling boards. Astute enough to foresee that, varnishing six hundred and fifty square feet of ceiling when it was in place would result in sleeves full of dripped varnish, I spread the packs of board around the hold and applied three coats whilst Peter slept in the mornings. It took a lot of mornings.

Between drying coats of varnish, with the saw Pete so generously bought for me, I cut hundreds of bits of timber into approximately sixteen inch lengths. That was the problem, if they had all been *exactly* sixteen inch lengths, my beloved Sandvik saw would have dismissed the task almost disdainfully. As it was, I had to measure each piece before hacking it off and wedging it between the angle iron roof beams whilst balanced on an old oil drum.

When Peter surfaced in the afternoon, fresh from sleep and eager to work, we really got to enjoy ourselves. We dressed up in big shirts and put chiffon scarves over our faces, held in place by woollen bobble hats. Gloves were positioned over elastic band held shirt cuffs and strips of sheeting filled the gap between turned up collars and bobble hats. Trousers trapped in knee high socks completed the ensemble and we focused chiffon glazed eyes on twenty rolls of fibre glass insulation.

Seven rolls at a time were laid across the floor and several feet of each roll were draped over a length of two by one timber. All I had to do – without so much as a beam me up Scottie – was leap onto my oil drum and hold this lot up to the roof whilst Peter fixed it in place. My arms, however, were neither long enough or strong enough to support this cumbersome burden above my head. I was going to need some help here. Help came, in the form of Peter's idea to prop one end up with a broom head attached to a length of timber. Most of our current stock of timber had been reduced to hundreds of approximately sixteen inch pieces, leaving only a couple of lengths that were nine inches too short to reach from floor to ceiling. A little blue stool, rendered surplus to sanitary requirements by a new low slung toilet, was brought into gainful employment to act as the missing nine inches.

With me and my oil drum propping up one end, and a broom handle fixed to a length of timber perched on a little blue stool propping up the other end, Peter was able, if he was quick, to wallop nails through his long piece of wood into my short bits. An exercise that was repeated many times before we reached the point by the front door. My arms reached the point of exhaustion long before the front door was reached. It took several sessions to complete this job, the end of each session being determined at the time my elbows sagged and Peter was clouted by two by one and draped in fibre glass.

Taking a break from inhaling fibre glass particles through chiffon, we postponed the fun of insulating the walls. A decision encouraged by the fact that the remaining rolls of insulation were in use as benches to hold varnished ceiling board. The order of things now was to release the rolls by nailing the boards to the timber holding the fibre glass up.

Banging hundreds of small nails upwards into the tongues of four inch wide ceiling boards proved to be almost impossible. Peter bought a Black and Decker staple gun, but our little Honda generator was not up to feeding this power hungry tool. When the trigger was pulled, the stapler sighed and spat just the tips of staples into the wood. A hammer still had to be applied to complete the fixing, but at least Peter wasn't swallowing nails anymore. The operation disturbed the fibre glass insulation above our heads, showering us with glittery particules, and we itched for days.

Peter had to explain his constant scratching when he became aware that work mates were moving away from him. One of them suggested baby oil. I think it would have been more valuable poured into the generator than on us.

Within a week, we had a ceiling over the area that was our potential bedroom. Being big on realising potential, I suggested that building a bedroom as the next project would relieve some of the problems of sleeping, cooking, eating and covering up parrots in the cramped confines of the aft quarters.

'If we were to line and insulate the walls of this area now,' I wheedled, 'we could construct a good sized bedroom.

Back to bobble hats, elasticated shirt cuffs and baby oil.

The trouble with living on a boat was that time had to spent on stuff that, in a former life, we never had to consider. For example, the cobbled together water tanks needed to be replenished once a month.

When we first arrived here, we'd seen ships moor by a concrete edifice that stood on land about a hundred and fifty yards in front of us. They appeared to be taking water, so we investigated.

Climbing up steps to a height of some twelve feet above ground level, we found a coin slot flanked by two push buttons. Looking over the top, we saw a dangling grey corrugated appendage that resembled a giant elephant's trunk.

Being in need of water, and not realizing that this equipment was designed to fill tanks belonging to large ships in a cargo carrying hurry, we made a mini voyage to the water point. A notice offered instructions – like all things in Belgium, be it washing powder or fish fingers – in two languages. A packet of flour on a Belgian supermarket shelf announced itself as farine on one side and as bloem on the other.

In this case, neither language was particularly useful, even to anyone who understood them. Most of the words, except the ones that indicated that a twenty franc coin must be placed in the slot, were partly obliterated. Presumably, bored bargee wives scratched at the notice with twenty franc coins whilst awaiting their husbands' instructions to push buttons. Not really a problem. The coin slot was obvious, and we assumed that one push button was for starting the flow of water and the other for stopping it. It couldn't be difficult.

It was ridiculously difficult! I went through several twenty franc coins trying to work out whether I should put the coin in first, then push the left hand button, or push the left hand button before putting the coin in. Or should I be pushing the right hand button? And, if so, should I do it before or after putting the coin in? Eighty francs was gobbled up before, by sheer chance, I hit on the permutation that resulted in a roar and a gigantic rush of water erupting out of the end of the hose Peter was holding, lifting him clear of the ground!

'Wonderful, Meg,' called a dripping Peter, 'Repeat exactly what you just did, but this time, wait until I've got the hose in position.'

The end of the hose was wider than our water fill hole. Peter placed the hose over the hole, applied all his weight to holding it down and yelled, 'Now.'

What I thought I had done before didn't work this time. I frantically shoved coins and pushed buttons. It was just as Peter released his grip to look up and ask what the hell I was doing, that I pushed the right button in the right sequence. This time, Peter was thrown backwards as a ton of water hit the deck and swirled over the roof like a manic tidal wave. No amount of thumping of either button was effective in stopping the flow. Once released, that ton of water was hell bent on escaping.

We conceded defeat when our tanks were half full of water and my pocket was empty of twenty franc coins.

In a mood befitting a man who is drenched and shivering, Peter manoeuvred an ultra clean barge back to it's mooring. The discovery that Colibri simply would not reverse in anything that came even near to suggesting a straight line did not enhance that mood.

'Next time we go for water, I'll wear a wet suit and have a go at turning this barge round,' said Peter morosely.

Before we went back to the water point, Peter manufactured an adapter to bring the end of the elephant's trunk down to the size of our filling hole. A tap positioned amid this assembly of ever decreasing sized pipes and fittings, that looked as if it expected some one to play a concerto on it, enabled Peter to regulate the flow of a ton of rampant water. I still swear that the abstrusely coded sequence of coin slotting and button pushing was reprogrammed monthly. A twenty franc ton of water invariably cost us at least sixty francs. I collected twenty franc coins with an avidity that suggested these mundane coins would, one day, become rare collectors' items.

In an effort to keep me in touch with the real world that winter, we sometimes went to the bar across the square in Zaventem. Mind you, I'm not at all convinced that the real world was to be found there, but it delighted me to see groups of teenage drinkers greet each other with handshakes for the boys, and kisses for the girls. An olde worlde courtesy that I had thought long gone.

As a woman, drinking in the male dominated company of Peter's work mates, I was often teased. I would smile smugly and chirrup, 'I don't care, 'cos I've got a Sandvik saw.'

'What do you know that the rest of us don't know?' asked a guy who had just bought a round of drinks when, for the second time that evening, I grabbed his change and sifted out the twenty franc coins.

Apart from these outings, I spoke to very few people. I was

busy; preoccupied with building my home, and occasions didn't often arise for me to make friends in a foreign country. We did have a Dutch sand barge as a regular neighbour. The barge was absolutely enormous, and was operated by a young husband and wife team; lovely people, shy and gentle. She was a very attractive blonde and he was knee bucklingly gorgeous. It was strange to see a pretty blonde lady driving a barge the size of a football pitch. Also funny to see their two kids playing with buckets and spades as an expanse of sand chugged down the canal; a mobile beach the size of which would accommodate a football team and their entire families in Benidorm. We would have liked to get to know this barge family better, but sadly, the language barrier frustrated chances of an easy friendship. We spoke no Dutch, and they were obviously shy and uncomfortable using their limited English with us.

George, however, had no such inhibitions. He was a retired Belgian bargee, born and brought up on the water. As a small child, at the end of the second world war, he'd travelled on his Father's barge when it was loaded with oranges from a big sea ship in Antwerp. The oranges were taken to France, and the return cargo was bodies of American soldiers in cloth bags. The bags were loaded onto ships in Antwerp and taken to America.

George went to school only when his parents' barge happened to be in Antwerp for a few weeks a year. So, how did he learn to speak English? Nowadays, he and his wife, Pauline, lived in a house and watched a lot of television. Their English was gleaned from English films with sub titles.

With total confidence, George nattered articulately, with complete disregard for grammar, tenses or anything else that got in the way of free flowing speech. Wonderful; we understood him, he understood us and a friendship developed. At first, Pauline was more reticent about speaking English, but she slowly overcame her shyness and we enjoyed the company of these very nice people. They were the first ones to congratulate us on aquiring a bedroom.

Yes, we did get one of those once the walls of that area were lined with fibre glass and clad with marine ply. Sounds really simple put like that. Actually, it was more like: How to to build an en suite bedroom in seventy one thought provoking stages.

A boat doesn't have any straight walls. It can have, if you

simply board in the sides from ceiling to floor, but we were determined to not only use all available space, but to retain the character of the barge. To both ends, we followed the inner line of the deck and hull.This took three times longer, but we ended up with a room that was three feet wider than if we had taken the easy route. Cupboards and water tanks were built into the under deck space. Also the toilet.

Positioning the toilet was fun. In fact, we were coming to accept that these hitherto unremarkable objects formed a large part of life's entertainment. Peter stood posed – but not exposed, I hasten to add – in a position for action, whilst I put my arms between his legs and moved the toilet around until Peter decreed it to be in the perfect position. Like numerous wives, I had stood in front of a television yelling: 'Yes!' 'No!' 'Nearly!' 'Good – blast, missed it!' whilst my husband adjusted a television aerial on a roof, but this joint effort toilet adjusting exercise was novel in our experience.

We then took it in turns to sit and stand to see if we could do so without clunking our heads on the under deck bit. I was severely reprimanded for moving the toilet during my turn at this activity, and we had to repeat the arms between legs positioning ritual.

Putting the first dividing wall up came close to being called fun as well. When there is not a single straight line to measure from, how the devil do you decide if a wall is exactly perpendicular, or at right angles to anything? The steel bulkhead between the engine room and the hold certainly wasn't exactly anything; couldn't take any sensible measurements from that. The side walls followed the shape of the hull, and the ceiling followed the lovely curve of the deck. That left the floor. It looked level, but we couldn't be sure. It was, however, the only thing that even approached a sensible angle, so we opted for the floor.

We then looked around for something to take a horizontal fix on. The top of the keel was just visible through the solid, tightly packed oak floor beams. It's curved top prevented it from breaking the Dutch Boat Builders' First Commandment, but it maybe violated it a bit by being dead centre and following an indisputably straight line fore and aft. We confidently placed our wall at right angles to it.

We assumed that we could line up all subsequent walls to this first one and that, if it did lean, then at least the rest of the construction would have a consistent lean. However, in accordance with the Creed, in the strict sense of the word, the floor was not exactly level throughout the boat. Therefore, compromise between what the tape measure said and what the eye saw determined future construction; with blatant disregard for conventional building disciplines. I believe that some of our interior walls are slightly closer together at ceiling height than at floor level. It all looks fine to us, and no one has ever said: 'By the way, did you know that your walls and doors lean?'

Reclining on a pine bed that, built with the aid of an accurate tape measure, required little blocks under the base to make the floor level, we celebrated our first night in our new bedroom with a bottle that was not hot or made of rubber. A bare light bulb hung from the ceiling and a precisely positioned loo eagerly awaited its shower and basin companions behind, what we hoped was, a precisely positioned bathroom wall.

What did it matter that we had no carpet, curtains or doors? We had our first room didn't we? It didn't seem to matter that we had to go through the wheelhouse and outside to climb through a metal deck hatch to go to bed.

Having an almost proper bedroom certainly improved our lives during the remainder of what was, in all honesty, a bloody difficult winter. The capricious little diesel brat was our only form of heating. A Honda, two kilowatt petrol generator served to charge batteries – incredibly noisily! It was put on the foredeck, as far away as possible, and run for three nerve rattling hours a day to provide sufficient battery power for lighting, hydrophore and my one weak indulgence – an electric blanket. The blanket was, of course, not twenty four volt, but two twenty volts. The magic conversion was brought about by an inverter; a bulky square wave affair that emitted a high pitched buzz that necessitated burying the thing under a pile of bed linen in a cupboard.

As winter moved towards spring, everything became easier. For a start, it took less time and energy to dress; and it's easier to work without layers of restricting clothing. The first evening that hinted at spring, we sat on deck drinking sundowners after a hard days work and congratulated ourselves. We felt that, by moving on board in mid winter and coping with the worst conditions, we had proved we were capable of full time living afloat. Things could only get easier from now on. Summer was coming, we were progressing well and, by next winter, Colibri would resemble something close to a comfortable home.

We raised faces to soft spring air, glasses to Colibri and emptied a wine bottle before taking a self satisfied stroll down the little leafy lane. On our return, we found that a lock operation had lowered the water by several feet. We had to jump from the wall down onto Colibri's roof, which was bobbing around like a demented cork. This was normal; we had become accustomed to this happening often. We knew by now that, after an average heave, it took about twenty minutes for our home to settle down again. In spite of these hazards, we had been happily tied to this wall for three months – or, more correctly, ninety lots of twenty four hours.

Chapter Six

BLOSSOMING

Before we were allowed to fall into spring complacency, we were treated to a reminder of how rough the weather could be. Not so much a gale, but a very strong wind attacked, out of the blue, one evening. Enough to make us tie the hatch down just in case.

Eating supper with the lights on, we thought we heard a voice shrieking above the wind. The voice sounded as if it was calling Colibri.

'I hate the wind,' I said. 'It plays tricks on my mind.'

'Well, this one is definitely out to get you. It's screaming at us!' exclaimed Peter, knocking my plate off the table in his haste to go above.

An unladen barge was hurtling towards us and a woman on deck was screaming: 'Colibri! Colibri!'

Assisted by a strong wind from behind, the barge slammed into Colibri. As it bounced off, Peter pointed to the rope clutched in the terrified woman's hand and managed to convey, with gestures that defied any language barrier, that she should get her rope across to him. Snapping out of shock induced paralysis, she hurled the rope. Peter caught it before the wind did, and secured it to one of our bollards. It was a struggle, involving a great deal of screamed words between the bargee and his wife in Flemish and between Peter and his wife in a language I won't define, but eventually the barge was brought safely alongside. Shivering, we returned to a cold supper, only to find the wind had extinguished the cute little diesel heater and filled the room with noxious smoke.

Up until then, the local bargees had been aloof and somewhat wary of us. They probably didn't understand who or what we were, so kept a safe distance. This barge had now been forced to make direct contact with *The Englishers*. For us, it was a break through. We had been able to display willingness to assist in an hour of need, and we were also able to reassure these people that the dent our rubbing strip made in their bow was not harmful to us. So, an invisible barrier began to topple and we began to become accepted.

These same people tied their barge alongside us several weeks later and asked if they could leave it in our care whilst they went to Antwerp to visit a sick parent. On another occasion, a different bargee asked if he could park his car beside us because he needed to leave it for a week. The wind that I hated so much, had presented a chance to break through to a group of regular neighbours.

Another plus of the winds was all those fallen trees. A gale always brought forth frenzied fuel collecting activity. Local people came with estate cars, trucks and trailers, and the strident hum of chain saws rent the air for days. We had considered buying a wood burning stove to install in our new living accommodation. All this free wood seemed to suggest that this was a good idea. We asked around, trying to find out if it was permitted for us to take the wood. The unvarying reply was: 'Yes, if nobody tells you not to.' This seemed to be quite a common criterion in Belgium. I'm sure there were lots of things, that maybe no hard and fast rules applied to, that you could do if nobody told you not to.

Like being moored where we were for more than twenty four hours for example.

Peter became quite excited about the prospect of tons of free fuel.

'When is your birthday?' he asked.

'Two weeks time,' I reminded him.

Peter bought me a chain saw for my birthday – two weeks early.

On the actual day, he took me to Zaventem to have a meal at our favourite Italian restaurant. Afterwards, we joined some of Peter's fellow workers at the bar across the square.

What took place was probably my own fault. I was never very good at swapping knitting patterns at all female coffee mornings. I am happier discussing the merits of an index finger as a tile grouting tool with other do-it-yourselfers, and Peter's work mates were used to my conversational topics.

Adrian arrived late and, in front of a group of eight men, proffered a cylindrical shaped parcel wrapped in vivid orange paper. It looked like the sort of item an Ann Summers Party hostess would deliver in a plain brown wrapper, and it bore the message: "Just a little something to amuse yourself with when

Peter is on night duty". My face the colour of the wrapping paper, I undid what proved to be the first of several layers of paper and toilet roll cardboard inners. Accompanied by a chorus of ribald comments, I worked my way through the multi layers until, with one layer left to go, my fingers came into contact with something I recognised.

'Oh goody!' I squealed, 'It's a tool!'

It was indeed a tool. It was the ratchet screwdriver I had longed for. I was genuinely delighted with Adrian's thoughtful gift, but I felt he should pay for the embarrassment he had subjected me to.

He hadn't counted on me kissing him in front of his work mates and saying: 'Thank you, Darling, you've made it possible for me to screw all day without getting blisters.'

For once, he didn't complain when I sifted through his change on the bar and swapped all the twenty franc coins for dozens of centimes. By that time, I had saved enough to buy myself a second hand bike for my birthday.

With the advent of full blown spring, life became extremely pleasant. The light evenings, warm weather and a normal sized – albeit not normal shaped – bedroom, all contributed to a contented, *aren't we lucky*! attitude.

Our poor little generator began to sigh with relief. It had worked much too hard – hadn't we all? – all winter to give us lights. I understood it's feelings; I too appreciated naturally lit evenings. I hated it less when Peter left for work and came home when it wasn't dark. Often, when he arrived home at seven a.m., he opened the bedroom hatch and called: 'Come and look at the day!'

Still sleepy and grumbling about not getting my cup of tea first, I stumbled up to the deck and looked at the day with him. Peace, tranquillity, early morning sun breaking through a light mist over the water; how could anyone ask for more? Peter found it hard to go to bed on days like that.

The fields beside us took on a pale green sheen, the trees that were still standing burst into life after their fraught winter and the little leafy lane was like a path through paradise. With the tree lined canal one side and deep woods the other, the lane led to the next village and a rather unexpected sign to a grott.

Wondering what on earth a grott was, we followed the sign to an open air church, with rows of benches set out like pews. Candles burned at an alter set into an outcrop of rock. A path led from this area, and a notice announced the twelve stations of the cross. Following the path, we came across twelve groups of statues depicting Christ's journey to Calvary and the scene of the Crucifixion, culminating in a tomb with a rolled away stone and three kneeling, weeping women. What an amazing and moving discovery, tucked away in a beautifully kept glade on the side of the canal. Although we were alone, we found ourselves speaking in hushed voices. The only other sound was the twittering and singing of birds in the surrounding woods.

Work inside became neglected with the weather encouraging us to tackle outside jobs. The new steel roof had been left to rust as instructed. Now all we had to do was scrub the rust off with a wire brush, coat it twice with red lead, twice with primer and twice with enamel top coat – all six hundred and fifty square feet of it!

Armed with a wire brush, Peter attacked a strip three foot long by eighteen inches wide. Looking like an orange faced red Indian, he stood back to survey his considerable effort. It was a mere scratch, hardly significant. He looked at the remaining six hundred and thirty five square feet and decided to do it next week – or the week after perhaps.

Rust is funny stuff, it stains skin. If you are heavily exposed to it, you end up resembling an item of teak furniture. We were heavily exposed to rust for two weeks.

On hands and knees, Peter looked a bit like an animated teak coffee table on a lead, moving sideways across the deck in slow motion. The lead being the cable of the electric drill that, with a round wire brush in the chuck, proved to be the most effective way to remove rust from steel. What we failed to find was an effective way to remove rust from people.

Once Peter had cleared an area, my job was to leap in with alacrity and red lead to catch it before it had a chance to consider re-growing a coat of fresh rust. Thus I became the rear guard coffee table, creeping close behind my leader with a pot of factor fifteen instant rust block.

Two hours at a time was all we could reasonably manage and still be able to stand up on two legs. With goggles and mouth mask removed, two red Indian teak tables became two white mouthed, owl eyed clowns. Colibri adopted the appearance of gaudy fairground equipment. The red lead clashed horribly with the rust, and as quickly as I could, I followed two coats of it with grey primer. Chequered stripes of grey, bright red and rust made their way down the roof as if an uncontrollable disease was taking over.

A similar disease assailed our bed linen and towels. Throwing a hand towel on the floor in disgust and grabbing a clean one to dry my face, I told Peter that it would be greatly appreciated if he would kindly wash his hands before he dried them.

'Does that go for your face too?' he asked, pointing to the pale rust coloured damp patches on the towel in my hand.

Unwilling to apply the wire brush treatment to skin and hair, we just sort of lived a rusty life until the job was finished. I'm sure we were eating the stuff.

Peter thought I needed a break from all that hard work – so he took me logging. My chain saw was a bright, shiny piece of serious looking machinery. Advised by a Croatian aircraft engineer-cum-lumberjack, Peter had gone for a heavy duty, petrol driven McCulloch. The sort that is more normally toted by massive shouldered, check shirted Canadians – or Croatians even.

Armed with this roaring, spitting instrument, Peter attacked fallen tree trunks the diameter of which needed a second bite from the eighteen inch chain. When the trunk was reduced to twelve or fifteen inch thick discs, I could just about lift one at a time. They were conveyed the hundred yards from the lumber site to the boat by jeep, then loaded on board and stacked in the potential dining room. All in four easy stages!

'You have a wood fire on your boat?' asked a local dog walker.

'No, not yet,' I replied.

The dog and the man walked off shaking their heads. Probably thinking: And they make jokes about the Belgians!

Light, warmer evenings meant more time enjoying being on deck and less time in the Zaventem bar. Peter's work mates, curious to take a look at this less than normal home of his, visited if they could find us. Peter told them we lived at Kappelle op den Bos. They said: "Where!" I believe it became established that we lived at that Kappelle whatsit place. A man that I wasn't acquainted with came, I think, to also take a look at this less than normal wife of Peter's. I knew he considered me odd when he told Peter that he was lucky to have a wife willing to go along with this scheme.

Why is it always assumed by men that other men doing anything with boats are only able to do so if they happen to be prudent enough to acquire a stupid or submissive woman? Surely this particular man could see that I was thrilled to be living in dungarees, knee deep in wood shavings, with jars of paint brushes in white spirit where other woman make do with vases of flowers.

He joined us for a meal cooked on the barbecue in the cargo hold. A sheet of ply wood balanced on bales of insulation pretended to be a table, and ill assorted plates were dumped in a bucket when we finished eating. The guy kept shaking his head and letting me know he couldn't wait to tell his wife about this.

Okay, so she's normal, I thought. No need to keep rubbing it in!

Mind you, I was upgraded to a level of slightly above that of a deranged saint when, visiting the aft quarters to see the parrots, this man discovered that I did have a sink and a cooker.

'It's nearly as good as the hotel I'm staying in', he commented. 'Why does that bird say "Petersh shleeping" in your wife's voice? Does she hit the bottle when you're in bed?'

I never did find out if he meant me or the parrot. He was on one of those two to three week contracts, and he disappeared after seven weeks. Probably to somewhere really boring where the sun shines quite often.

Working inside again during a rainy week, we heard some one knocking on the wheelhouse door. Going up to investigate, Peter found two grubby little boys. One of them spoke a bit of English and, between odd words of this and some even odder words of Flemish, he managed to convey that they wanted to wash their bikes. With our bucket on a rope, Peter fished up some canal water, gave the boys a scrubbing brush and left them to it. Later, we heard knocking on the hull and I went up to find two rather agitated little boys.

The smaller one hopped from one foot to the other. The slightly larger one pointed to where our bucket was floating down the canal in the general direction of Brussels. I pretended to be very angry. Scowling at Larger one, I said, 'What? You've lost my bucket!'

'He,' said Larger one, backing off and pointing to his smaller companion.

I turned to Smaller one with an expression of outrage. Poor little sod, he didn't know it was feigned outrage. He didn't know what I had said either, but he understood the tone in which it was said. His already white face blanched to a deeper shade of ashen beneath the mud pack. Eyes stared at me; huge beacons of reflected terror.

Instantly contrite, I dropped my fierce pose, took his little hand, smiled and said, 'Neen probleem.' I'm not sure he grasped my attempt at Dutch, but he realized he was off the hook. Suspended breath escaped in a tremulous *Phew!* The hand I held squeezed mine, the other one swept his brow, and I watched two huge eyes reduce to a normal size.

Strange, these Belgian kids. Why on earth didn't they just scarper instead of attracting our attention so they could confess? Disquieting to think that we would have considered that more normal.

By upgrading my collective urge to fifty franc coins, I was able to present Peter with a second hand bike by the end of April. Enjoying this slow pollution free mode of travel, we took advantage of evenings when Peter didn't go to work and explored around.

We met Frank and Gina in a bar. It was Frank's fortieth birthday and they were celebrating with some fellow American friends. We only popped in for cigarettes, but they insisted that we join them for a drink. 'Just one,' we said.

'Where'sh the car?' asked Frank when we left the bar four hours later.

'In the square,' said Gina.

We assisted them to the square and refereed an argument precipitated by Frank giving Gina the car keys.

'Your turn to drive!' said Gina.

'Can't – too sloshed,' said Frank.

'You'll have to. I can't even see the car!'

'S'over there. Drive me home, woman!'

Gina tried to fit a rubber Snoopy key holder into the lock. 'Do you know,' complained Gina, 'there are seven red lights between here and home?!'

'Sure,' replied Frank, 'But we don't have to stop at every police station do we?'

He stretched out on a bench and promptly fell asleep. Peter put the car keys in Gina's handbag and put Gina in a taxi. The taxi drove round the square and came back. We picked Frank up and put him in the taxi. Peter went round to the other side and put Gina back into the taxi.

The taxi drove round the square and came back.

'Where to?' the driver asked. 'They don't know.'

We found a card with an address on it in Gina's handbag. We hoped it was hers. The taxi drove off and we picked Frank up and put him in another taxi. The first taxi drove round the square and came back.

'Lost a passenger!' said the driver.

'Follow that cab,' said I.

'Our lights haven't got bikes,' announced Peter, and sat cross legged on the ground. I picked him up and put us both in a taxi.

'Do you speak English?' I asked the driver.

'Yes, I'm Dutch,' he replied.

'Really? What's a Dutchman doing driving a taxi in Belgium?'

'Earning a living. Where to?'

'Doppelle den sen bosh.'

'Where?'

'Boppel kop bon des.'

The driver turned round in his seat, focused on my lips and said, 'Try again.'

I closed my eyes, put my fingers in my ears and said, 'Kap -pel-la . . .'

'Op den bos,' supplied the driver.

'Gotcher!' I said.

The driver woke me up and said, 'Where to now?'

'Bokelle . . .'

'No, not that bit. We're at Kappelle op den Bos, where do you live?'

'Colibri.'

'You live in Colibri?'

'*On* Colibri.'

'I see, where is this colibri?'

'In the canal.'

The driver lit a cigarette, took a deep breath and said, 'So, you live on a colibri in the canal – have I got that right?'

'S'right.'

'Lady, you can live in a house, in a barn, a tent or even a damn great chateau if you like – you can't live on a little bird!'

'I *do*. S'barge.'

'A *what*!

'BARGE!

He apologised for shouting at me and said that he fully understood. 'So, you live on a barge, it's called Colibri, and it's in the canal – right? Which side of the canal?'

'My side. Our side. I don't know. Which side are we on?'

'You're sure as hell not on my side! Look, do me a favour, please just try and tell me where your Colibri is.'

'It's two hundred yards from the elephant's trunk.'

'Of course it bloody is – I should have guessed!'

Summer began to poke it's fingers into our souls and make us restless. Peter planned to take a month's leave in July; we itched to go cruising. An itch that no amount of baby oil could placate, but we kept the baby oil in anticipation of summer cruising sunburn. We had worked and struggled our way through a difficult winter; it was nearly time to jog this big black monster of ours into doing what it was supposed to do. It was nearly time to go cruising – and the weather was beckoning.

June was hot, but there seemed to be a breeze and a freshness ever present on the water. We looked forward to fresh breezes created by a moving boat. Abandoning construction work, we prepared Colibri for travelling. Our rusty tramp ship began to disappear under layers of gleaming paint. Peter thought his wife was doing likewise. A few early pleasure boats passed by. We waved paint streaked hands and longed to join them.

I filled the food cupboard in preparation for our voyage. With burning sun beating down on my head, I loaded cans and packets from a supermarket trolley into the jeep. The driving seat scalded my bare legs as I climbed into a yellow Dhaihatsu oven. It would be nice to leave the jeep behind and just go off in a ventilated wheelhouse.

I had gazed longingly through the window of a shop that sold shiny mopeds. Peter thought we should have one, but I pointed out that we could buy a cast iron wood burning stove for a similar price. So I shopped for food as if we were going to be out of touch with supermarkets for a month. I did buy a sun umbrella with the fifty franc coins left over from buying Peter's bike.

The day before Peter's leave began, a lovely little Luxe Motor barge moored at the wall in front of us. The elderly Dutch couple on board told us they were cruising to France. We delighted in the fact that we wouldn't be far behind them.

It was a beautiful summer evening. Whilst we ate dinner on deck, two of Peter's colleagues arrived. I fetched another bottle of wine and waved at the elderly Dutch couple who were setting off for a stroll down the little leafy lane. Dave, another engineer, arrived just as the Dutch couple returned from their stroll.

A very enjoyable evening on deck in pleasant company. It was good to see Peter beginning to relax. But, he was not on holiday until tomorrow, and at nine o'clock, he and two of our guests left to go on night duty. Peter kissed me goodnight, and the other two men kissed me goodbye and wished me happy cruising. Dave waved smugly from his chair beside the anchor winch. He was off duty that night, and we sat chatting until he left just before midnight; complaining bitterly because we were taking the boat away for a month.

In the morning, I was wide awake, contentedly watching sparkling water reflections dance across the bedroom ceiling when I heard Peter leap on board just after seven.

'Come and look at the day!' he yelled.

Without even grumbling about cups of tea in bed, I scrambled out of the duvet and joined Peter on deck. We looked at the day together. It was a glorious day – and we had a whole month of freedom ahead.

Refusing to waste the first morning of his holiday by going to bed, Peter had breakfast on deck then announced that he had some shopping to do. He wasn't gone long, and a huge grin split his face in two when he returned, leapt from the jeep and opened the rear door.

'Pressie!' he said, unloading a bright shiny blue moped.

Between my hugs and kisses, he explained that it was an essential piece of boat equipment. Road transport that we could carry on board – in lieu of a Lotus Elan.

In the afternoon, we shopped some more and called in at the Zaventem bar. Glen pounced on us as we were sipping cold beer at an umbrella shielded pavement table.

'I've just driven over to your place. You weren't there,' Glen complained.

'No, mate, we're here,' said Peter. 'Want a beer?'

Through gulps of cold beer, Glen told of how he had driven up to Colibri, gone on board and, finding nobody home, had approached the barge moored in front.

'The old Dutch woman was a bit odd,' said Glen. 'Before I had a chance to speak, she opened her wheelhouse door, said – rather sharply, I thought – "The Frau is not there!" and closed her door. What have you done to her, Meg? She doesn't seem very friendly.'

'That's odd,' I replied. 'She was fine yesterday when . . . Oh hell!'

I gawped at Glen in open mouthed horror as realization crashed like a ton of metal filings. 'It's all those men!' I said, 'Three last night – four including Peter – coming and going. Then you this morning. What the hell is she thinking?'

Peter and Glen thought they knew exactly what she was thinking. They also thought it was very amusing. I did not!

'I'll have to try and explain somehow,' I wailed.

When we got back home, the elderly Dutch couple and their lovely little Luxe Motor had gone.

'Can't say I blame them,' chortled Peter. 'You're hardly a suitable neighbour for a respectable elderly couple.'

'Who cares?' I grinned back. 'The sun is shining, we're on holiday, and I feel like a loose abandoned woman.'

'May I remind you,' said Peter, 'that I haven't been to bed since yesterday morning?'

Chapter Seven

FIRST STEPS ALONE

Neither of us felt inclined to eat breakfast in the morning. We were nervous, in fact, we were very, very nervous at the prospect of taking our ropes off and leaving our nice safe wall.

The plan was to leave about ten o'clock. About nine thirty, I said, 'Peter, you know that flag that all the ships have?'

'Which flag?'

'Those ones on the front. Red, with a white square in the middle. What does it mean?'

'It means,' replied Peter, 'that you have to make one before we travel.'

He had overlooked the fact that it was obligatory for any boat moving in Belgian waters to fly the red and white flag at the bow. We must have one before we entered Brussels.

My box of fabrics was still in England. I hadn't exactly had time for sewing recently, and I searched for something red. In a canvas bag under the aft quarters bed, I found – would you believe? – a thermal vest! Rummaging deeper, I came up with a red tee shirt. A square cut from this, smaller squares from an old white sheet, some hasty stitching and – voila! – we had the required piece of kit.

A visit to the elephant's trunk for a top up, and we were on our way. Knowing that our first obstacle was a lifting bridge, and not knowing how to get it lifted, we waited for some ships to leave the lock and tagged on behind. Five miles of wide canal to practise in before having to tackle the Brussels complex.

Brussels is the end of the line for the very big ships; the locks become much smaller, and hold just two sixteen foot wide boats side by side. Three barges waited to enter the first lock. We waited while two of them passed through; then it was our turn. It would have been nice to wait until the barge in front had settled in the lock before Peter squeezed Colibri into the space beside it. A space that looked narrower than Colibri. But procrastination, not to mention dithering, is heavily frowned upon. Other barges were appearing behind us. These were tough guys we were in amongst; commercial shippers with cargoes to deliver.

A man on the lockside beckoned impatiently and, with an intake of breath reminiscent of our first lock with Tiger Lily, Peter entered the lock. The impatient beckoner lowered a piece of string with a hook on the end as, once again, I clutched a handful of rope that I wasn't sure what to do with. I couldn't see any bollards – floating, sinking or otherwise. Violent jerking of the hook endowed string swinging close to my face brought realization that I was supposed to put my rope on the hook. Once this was accomplished, the rope was hauled up and placed on a bollard on land. We rose to ground level.

Next came the paperwork. I was told to report to the lock office with the ship's *meetbrief* (log book). I duly trotted up a lot of steps and presented our credentials.

'Where is the Port of Registry?' I was asked. I pointed to the entry in the *meetbrief*. 'That is in Holland,' said the officious man.

'Yes,' I said. 'The ship is Dutch registered.'

'But, you are speaking English,' he informed me.

'That's because I am English.'

'The proprietor of the ship, is he Dutch?'

'No, he is British.'

'But, the ship has a Dutch flag.'

'That's because the ship is Dutch registered.' I was getting fed up with this. What was wrong with this man? Wasn't he satisfied that a dissected red tee shirt flapped obligatorily from our bow? Barges were piling up outside the lock, waiting for us to leave so they could come in. Our lock partner, with thrashing propeller, had steamed off to the next lock. Pointless really, he would have to wait for us to join him before he could pass through.

'You must pay twenty francs,' I was told. No problem, I had a few of those. With a Gallic type shrug and some exasperated head shaking, the official heavily stamped some papers and thrust them into my hand. I was dismissed and we went on our way.

At each lock, I trotted up several flights of steps to present our papers. At each lock, a rubber stamp was applied. We didn't understand this. We had been recorded on entering the first lock, we couldn't escape or disappear; why was it necessary to delay our and all the other barges' progress by going through this tiring procedure of recording our passage through each lock? I was on holiday, taking a break from lifting tree trunks and wielding lumps of timber, but these guys with their endless steps were determined to keep my waistline on the run.

After six locks, we were clear of Brussells, and we were pretty well exhausted. Peter had coped well with the strain of manoeuvring a cumbersome vessel in and out of locks and through narrow passages. Being a novice bargee among throttle bashing professionals is nerve wracking. No doubt he would be fine after a few weeks practice, but right now, he needed a rest.

Before leaving the seventh lock, Peter asked if it was permitted to moor at the wall just beyond the gates. He was told that it was permitted, but not wise. The lock keeper explained that, quite often when barges moored there, they were hit by other barges.

'You must understand,' he said, 'that not all barge drivers enter the locks as easily as you.'

Our amusement at this incongruous statement eased tension, and we trundled on to find somewhere safe to moor for the night. Elated at our first day of freedom, we spent our first night away from base at a sand quay in a very pretty setting, out of sight of our next significant hurdle.

Ronquieres inclined plane lay just round the bend. Why were we worried about this? Who knows? It just sounded complicated. After breakfast, I gallantly declared my intention to go and suss this one out. Peter was going to have to negotiate this unusual canal equipment; the least I could do was find out exactly what was in store for him.

Peter was on the foredeck, anxiously awaiting the return of his intrepid bicycling wife. 'What did you see?' he asked as I pedalled into view.

'Two things,' I replied, braking to a halt – I must try to remember that continental bikes have opposing brake levers – 'Firstly, the plane looks just like any other lock. Nothing to it, except there's a stack of other boats waiting to go up. Secondly, the elderly Dutch couple's Luxe Motor is there. I waved, but they didn't wave back.'

I didn't actually know which of these two pieces of information caused Peter to grin like an idiot.

On arrival at the base of the plane, we reported in. Colibri's dimensions were given, a calculator was employed and we were told that we should enter the chamber for the third operation of the day; at approximately four thirty in the afternoon. It was explained which boats would enter in which order. One of the boats listed with us was the little Dutch Luxe Motor. Neighbours again – and I had several hours in which to rescue my reputation.

I did it quite casually. I strolled up to the lady and said, 'Hello, nice to see you again. My HUSBAND and I were hoping to catch up with you. We wanted to have a chat with you the other night, but my HUSBAND'S COLLEAGUES called on US to wish us a happy holiday.

They were really nice people. Gave us coffee and showed us over their boat, which they were, justifiably, very proud of. We showed them our barge and said that we hoped it would one day be as nice as theirs. They told us they lived on board, in a peaceful little inlet somewhere near Amsterdam. Although both in their seventies, they cruised for a couple of months each year.

We enjoyed their company whilst awaiting out turn to ride the inclined plane, which is an impressive piece of engineering. Normal looking lock gates opened and boats went into a large tank affair. Instead of the water rising or lowering like a normal lock, the whole tank full of boats is lifted to the canal above. On two hundred and thirty six wheels, the tank rises two hundred and thirty feet in a little less than a mile. We watched, fascinated, as boats were packed and despatched. It was a bit like witnessing Newton's apple and the Eureka syndrome with the Barrel of Bricks after dinner speech thrown in for good measure.

At last, it was our turn to ride in the magic bucket. Following the prescribed order, we entered last. The calculator had got it's sums wrong. We were supposed to go alongside a German barge – but one of us was too wide! The controller was insistent that we could fit in – it was his calculator – and some easing, squeezing and grunting took place until, slightly askew, with our bow tucked beside the German barge's stern, we were just about in sufficiently for the gates to be closed. This was actually happening when two Dutch motor boats decided to join us.

We had seen the two boats arrive on the scene within the last half hour, and had assumed that, like everyone else, they would book in and join the queue. They, however, had other ideas. One of them shot in beside our stern; the other one tried to follow suit, but there wasn't quite enough space. Believe it or not, having patiently waited seven hours for our turn, we were told to reverse out to let the motor boats in in front of us.

Reverse! Ho, ho, ho! Colibri does not go backwards. Well, she does, but not in the normally accepted straight line sort of manner, and she was already askew in a confined space. The first motor boat was dangerously close to our stern – a stern that would swing across as soon as reverse gear was brought into the action of a moving barge. The seventy plus year old Luxe Motor man took a rope astern, and Colibri was part motored and part manhandled out of the tank. The second motor boat, with haste taking priority over sense, shot in through a small gap, playing dodgems between our moving stern, the companion motor boat and the German barge's bum. The whole process of fitting Colibri into the tank was re enacted, and I just had time to snatch our flagstaff off before it was trapped in the closing gates.

An hour later, we were at the top. Emulating James Hunt leaving a pit stop, dodging round the German barge instead of waiting for it to move out ahead of them, the two motor boats roared out of the tank and disappeared.

We left the tank, motored across to a row of bollards and settled down for the night, having travelled something like five miles that day.

At seven thirty next morning, we were woken by the roar of familiar sounding high speed engines and the jabber of the same Dutch voices of yesterday. Obviously these impatient travellers didn't actually want to go anywhere – it was just fun to ride up and down the plane. The tank gates were still open from their hasty departure the previous evening, and the two devil helmed motor yachts were belting towards them. Fortunately – sorry, I mean *Un*fortunately – someone saw them coming. The gates closed when the two boats were a mere ten feet or so from entering. They screamed into reverse and we saw, with some satisfaction, that motor yachts aren't happy about going backwards either. Bouncing off each other, then disentangling themselves from each other's many rubber fenders, they took to the bollards in front of us. They were still there – awaiting their turn perhaps? – when we left at eleven o'clock.

That was our first encounter with the high speed clog contingent. It wasn't our last. We had always had a fondness for the Dutch, but we came to understand that, at the helm of a motor yacht, they grew horns.

We had wondered at the fastidiousness of a lady whose barge, coming from the opposite direction, moored across from us at the top of the Ronquieres Plane the night before. The lady had spent an hour fishing up buckets of water and scrubbing her decks.

At Charleroi, we turned left onto the River Sambre and into a lock. A blast furnace beside the lock belched out voluminous clouds of ash and black smoke. By the time we locked through, we and Colibri were covered in a thick film of the stuff. That night, moored in an idyllic setting, we too scrubbed our decks; aided by pouring rain.

Gliding smoothly down the Sambre as if we hadn't a care in the world, we arrived at Namur. 'I reckon I'm getting the hang of this,' said Peter, bringing Colibri easily and gently alongside a wall. I agreed as I nonchalantly plopped ropes on bollards that sat docilely awaiting me right beside the barge.

'Easiest mooring yet,' I said, pouring us both a mooring up drink.

A barge very similar to ours arrived. The driver pulled in behind us with practised aplomb, impressing us by leaving the wheel and stepping out of the wheelhouse to say, 'Hi,' as he passed. But a guy on the foredeck was clutching a handful of rope and wearing a *what do I do with this rope?* sort of look that I recognised, so I leapt ashore and bollard plopped his rope for him.

The owner of the barge, an Australian, was a friend of our diminutive Belgian neighbour. 'You must know Tom and Christine as well,' he said.

No, we didn't know Tom and Christine. Apparently, they were fellow Brits and lived on a Luxe Motor in Liege. Apparently, everyone knew them – except us.

Namur, or Namen, depending on whether you're speaking to Walloon or Flemish Belgians, is a nice town. We prowled around a big open air market and I fell in love with a crate of kittens. I resisted the enormous temptation to buy one, based on the fact that I knew a pregnant cat in Kappelle op den Bos. I also resisted the opportunity to ride by cable car to the high above citadel. Not difficult, I'm terrified of lifts even.

During dinner that evening, thinking that Peter was rather preoccupied, I asked what was on his mind.

'To be honest, Meg, I don't actually know how to get out of here.'

I could understand his anxiety. When we had moored here, there was plenty of room. Now, however, we had a barge behind and a small plastic boat almost touching our bow. We not only needed to get out, but to then make an immediate turn into the River Meuse.

'We could wait until the other boats have moved away,' was my faint hearted suggestion.

'Not good enough,' said Peter. 'I have to be able to handle this boat. I just need time to work it out.'

He worked it out, in theory. He pulled it off in practice, but I confess to being extremely jittery as he, first brought the stern out from the wall, then brought the bow past the plastic boat before swinging into about a hundred and forty degree turn to enter the River Meuse.

'How did you do that?' I asked in admiration.

'I think I know. And I hope I can do it again,' was the terse reply.

After Namur, some breathtaking scenery kept my camera busy. Passing through a spectacular gorge with sheer cliffs rearing up to a thousand feet above river, we cruised on to the delightful citadel town of Dinant. Another must for an overnight and some exploring. We moored directly beneath the citadel and enjoyed a warm evening on deck with a backdrop of the citadel and a magnificent church floodlit to display a scene of splendour. This longed for cruise was proving to be an absolute delight. The Meuse Valley was fabulous, and the French Ardennes lay ahead.

At Givet, the first French town after the Belgian/French border, we tried to report our presence in France. There was no one at home at the Customs Office. Peter found a River Navigation Authority office, told them we were here and enquired about the height of the Ham tunnel we were to negotiate. He was assured that the height of our wheelhouse was no problem.

After spending a couple of nights in Givet, we moved on.

Partly because a church clock not only struck every quarter of an hour, but also played the tune of Three Blind Mice. It was affecting our sleep pattern at night and threatening to blow our minds!

We entered the lock that preceded the Ham Tunnel. The lock keeper looked up at our wheelhouse and said, 'Peut-etre.' Which basically meant maybe we would get through the tunnel, but probably not. Once the lock was down, it was obviously a case of the latter. We were too high to pass under the lock bridge. We couldn't even leave the lock, let alone navigate the tunnel directly beyond it!

Faced with no alternative but to dismantle the wheelhouse or back out of the lock and go back to Belgium, we dismantled the wheelhouse. Off came the roof panels, then the hinged windows were folded down. Looking like a peeled banana, Colibri left the lock and entered the tunnel. It was so nice to have an al fresco wheelhouse, that we decided to keep it that way. Whilst the sun shone anyway.

The sun shone. We passed through the Revin tunnel and revelled in the fact that we were in France in glorious weather. Belgian officialdom was left behind; the French lock keepers had a laid back attitude and no steps for me to climb. They were simply not interested in our paperwork. They weren't too fussed about procedures either.

We knew from our chart, as well as a lifetime of traffic dicipline, that we must wait for a red light to change to green before we entered a lock. We knew that sort of basic stuff from our civilized experience of Brentwood High Street. Waiting outside a lock for a red light to change to green, we saw a lock keeper beckoning us in. When we were alongside him, he asked why we had waited – after all, his gates were open and ready to welcome us. Peter explained that his traffic lights were rouge. He shrugged and explained that the lights had been broken for months.

'But,' Peter pointed out, 'our book say's we are not permitted to enter a lock if a red light shows.'

'This is important!' The man was fascinated to see printed information on his lock. 'How many people have this book?' he asked.

'All boats have it.' Peter told him.

We accepted the man's apologies. He accepted a beer and told us we could moor for the night just beyond his lock. It was a beautiful place, and we felt inclined to go along with that suggestion.

'There is one bollard,' said the lock keeper. 'I will show you.'

He walked into some long grass and pointed, taking my rope to place it on a well hidden bollard. A metal stake banged into the bank acted as a second rope holder, and we enjoyed a mooring up drink in the early evening sunshine.

'Is this as good as you hoped it would be?' I asked Peter.

'Nope. It surpasses my dreams,' he replied.

After closing his lock for the day, the keeper came with a scythe and cleared the long grass beside Colibri. 'I keep the bollard hidden,' he explained. 'So the Dutch don't see it.'

We basked in this bias based privilege, and the lock keeper enjoyed another couple of beers with us until, from the lock cottage, his wife emitted a shriek worthy of a Billingingsgate wife to let him know that his dinner was going cold.

Before nine in the morning, a team of men had turned up to repair the lock lights. When we left an hour later, they were happily experimenting with different coloured sequences. The lock keeper waved, beamed and proudly pointed to his newly flashing beacons.

Nearly half way through July; nearly halfway through our month of liberty. We looked for somewhere really nice to spend a few days before turning round to go home. We found a beautiful place, just before the Joigny lock, five or six miles from Charleville-Mezieres. Passing a rope round overhanging, shade offering trees, we clambered off the boat and into a riverside meadow. High hills, mountains really, rose up on the opposite bank. Superbly idyllic! Colibri's bow was tucked into the curve of a tree trunk and densely leafed branches hung over part of the deck and formed a shady roof over the dismantled wheelhouse. From the bank, it looked more like a crash landing than a controlled mooring. A few sheep came and peered at us, then ran off bleating derisively.

Needing bread, we excused ourselves to the sheep and walked across their meadow and along a track to the village. The boulangerie was closed, so we sat at a bar's pavement table and enjoyed a glass of cold white wine while waiting for the afternoon batch of fresh bread to materialize.

I decreed it to be too hot to cook indoors, so a barbecue was lit and we ate outside, sitting under the parasol I had so wisely indulged in, and watched the sun sink behind the hills. If we had ever had any doubts about the wisdom of buying this barge, they would have been dispelled there and then.

Lunching on fresh bread and cheese under trees next day, we watched a self drive hire boat approach the lock. The people on board waved, and we waved back and yelled at them that the lock was closed for lunch. They brought their boat alongside us and we secured it to our deck bollards. Two French families, with four children, were on board. Noticing the children staring at the parrots in their cage on the tree shaded deck, I invited them to take a closer look. Once parental approval had been gained, the kids scrambled onto Colibri and sat cross legged in front of the cage. Dillon said, 'Excuse me,' and proceeded to entertain by singing: 'La, la, la,' whilst swaying from side to side.

One of the men in the party spoke excellent English and translated the many questions the women were asking about the barge. I suggested that they go inside and see for themselves. One woman walked down the steps from the foredeck, peeped into the hold, popped her head up and said something which made the man laugh.

'What did she say?' I asked.

'She said "They live in paradise",' he told me.

'Paradise!' I squeaked. 'You should see down there; it's full of tree trunks!'

'It is possible to make very nice furniture from tree trunks,' he commented politely.

'No, you don't understand. Our furniture is not *made* from tree trunks. Our furniture *is* tree trunks – complete with bark and oozing sap!'

The other man in the group spoke no English. His name was Michelle, and he was very French. In fact, he went all over the barge saying: "*Ooh la la*". That was the first time I realized that French people really do say *Ooh la la*. I had always thought it was just an exaggerated way to portray the French in television programmes like *Allo, Allo*.

The children were still sitting, mesmerised, in front of the parrots' cage when the lock re-opened after lunch. Dillon was giving a heartfelt rendering of Pop Goes the Weasel when the kids were instructed to re-board their own boat. Each child solemnly shook my hand and said "*Merci Madame*".

We cast them off and they drifted away with many calls of *Au revoir* and *Bon voyage*. One of the ladies waved a bottle in our direction, Michelle grabbed it and threw it across the widening gap. They applauded when I caught it and again when Peter caught me before I fell in the river. The entire party was yelling "*Merci. Merci beaucoup*".

'And Merci beaucoup to you to,' muttered Peter when he looked at the impressive label on the champagne bottle in my hand. 'But I reckon we should let it settle after being tossed through space before we open it and blow our heads off.'

Intrigued by the French lady's suggestion that we lived in paradise, I wondered what she had seen as she so briefly cast a glance into our home – potential home even – that suggested life in paradise? Trying to be objective, as if I had never looked in there before, I walked down the front steps and gazed into the hold.

I'm blowed if I could see what she meant! Before my eyes was a disorganized building site!

That night, or rather, in the early hours of the morning, I woke up, disturbed by brilliant moonlight flooding the bedroom. I went up onto the deck and looked at a stunning starlit sky. The river, hills and trees were eerily bathed in the silver fluorescence of a full moon. Without the interference of street lights, or even house lights, I was gazing at pure, unadulterated beauty.

'Come and look at the night,' I called to Peter.

With a pot of tea, we sat under the umbrella of overhanging branches. 'Tell you what,' I said, 'I reckon we live in paradise.'

This was what it was all about. This was the life we envisioned for ourselves in a few years time. A grassy bank, trees overhead; removed from the pressures of modern day living. In the next day or two, we would have to turn our barge round and go back to Kappelle. We had to continue to build our home and Peter must go back to work. Meanwhile, we treasured our dreams and the blissful tranquillity of here and now.

We hadn't allowed for the high speed clog lot!

The locks closed at eight in the evening. The evening of July 13th, they closed for Bastille Day until the 15th. At two minutes to eight on the said 13th, two Dutch motor yachts screamed up to the lock. Forget it, chum, gestured the lock keeper. His lock was closed.

Two boats circled around, the occupants yelling across to each other. With sinking hearts, we saw them pointing to the trees in front of us. So, we thought we had got ourselves a peaceful Bastille Day? So, we were wrong!

For most of the day that was a public holiday in remembrance of the start of a bloody revolution, seven kids, well trained by go faster parents, roared up and down the river in two outboard motor endowed dinghies. By evening, they were bored with this activity, so they played high decibel vocal football in the sheep's meadow.

Thankfully, true to form, the two boats were hooting at the lock ten minutes before opening time next day. Peace settled again, and we stayed another day just to enjoy paradise revisited.

Of course, one of the joys of living on a boat is that, if you don't like your neighbours, you simply move. In those early days, however, moving Colibri around at whim didn't seem that simple to us. It was some time before we treated mooring and unmooring as a casual event. At that point in time, Peter had only once turned this barge around since we'd had it.

He did it for the second time when, reluctantly, we began our return journey. The few days rest had been wonderful, and Peter was feeling relaxed and more confident about handling his barge. I also felt more relaxed, and I stretched out on deck under my sun umbrella.

We passed through Montherme, waving back at people waving at us from other boats. It's funny how strangers on boats wave at each other. We don't do it from cars, do we? I was pondering this when a gust of wind caught my umbrella, turned it inside out and dumped it in the river. People on the bank yelled and pointed. I grabbed the boat hook, but too late. The river claimed my brolly in seconds.

Peter knew I had saved housekeeping francs for that umbrella and he was more upset than I was. I think some of the spectators on shore were more upset than I was. I acknowledged their sympathetic waves and shrugs as we glided past.

Coming out of the lock cut at Dinant, we spied a mooring wall across the river. A boat was already moored there, and the wall looked inviting. Peter swung Colibri across, got caught by the strong river current and realized he had made a mistake. A bumper gust of wind taken broadside and we were in trouble. The only thing to do to stop us being swept sideways down river was to push on lots of forward power and try to turn up into the current.

On the foredeck, watching us head, very quickly, for the moored boat, I screamed. Just as I was convinced we were going to smash into the other boat, Colibri swung in front of it and hit the wall, knocking me off balance. I scrambled to my feet in time to see our stern squash one of the other boat's fenders. Then we were clear and going alongside the wall. Gasping with relief, I threw a rope onto a bollard then yelled at Peter, 'How the *** did you manage not to crush that boat!'

'I'm ***ed if I know,' he replied. I noticed the tremor in his voice.

Peter realized, afterwards, that in those few fraught minutes, he had learned more about how to handle the barge than in the two weeks he had been driving it. A sort of crash course in barge handling you might say. We also learned not to under estimate river currents – and that, if you are going to hit another boat, pick one with no people on it. It was fortunate that our moored up target was unoccupied. Anyone on board would have been scared witless!

A mooring up drink restored our calm, and Peter, having spotted a D.I.Y. shop across the river, took the moped off to go and have a look. I expected him to return with screws or door knobs. He came back with a new sun umbrella.

I felt nervous again when we set off next day. Peter, on the other hand, felt that he had really gained from our near disaster. Just as well; as we neared a lock, the gates opened and a herd of motor yachts stampeded towards us. One from the rear of the lock tried to be first out; dodging and overtaking inside the lock.

Eight boats were bearing down on us from all directions. Most looked like passing us on the wrong side. One small boat hung back from the herd and looked as if it would pass on the correct side.

'I'm going for the majority,' Peter said. 'Blue flag the last one to let him know we're passing him on his starboard side.'

I brandished the blue flag and the little boat changed sides. As he passed us, the skipper saluted and called, "Thanks". Bless him, he was flying a Red Ensign.

We had to wait in the lock whilst a large steel Dutch cruiser disentangled itself from the buzzing flotilla before it could join us. The driver was waving at his compatriots – his fist, not his hand.

Accompanying me on my multi-step paperwork trek, the Dutch cruiser man said, 'Those mad bloody Dutch! In Holland, we call them the Tupperware Fleet. They are all determined to get there first.'

'Where?' I asked.

'No one knows. They don't know, but they all want to get there as fast as possible. I saw you lose your umbrella, I was sad for you.'

'Thank you. My husband bought me a new one.'

We spent an enjoyable evening with this man and his wife in Namur before turning once again into the River Sambre. A nice spot we had noticed on our outward journey had attracted us, and we planned to stop there for the night on our way home. It was a *very* nice spot. Three bollards on a little wall at the edge of woods.

We tramped through the woods and I collected a potato net full of firewood. 'For our first fire when we get our stove,' I told Peter. He thought it would be nice, in winter, to remember our summer cruise with the contents of my potato net.

From a converted barge that was moored on the other side of the river, a man called across and invited us to have a drink with them. Another nice idea, but we couldn't see how to get to the road so we could cross over the bridge to the other barge.

'How do we get to you?' I called.

'Through the bus-shes,' he called back.

So, we fought our way through the bus-shes and shared some rather nice French wine with Noel and Nellie. He French, she Belgian.

'You have a Dutch flag on your boat,' said Noel.

'That's because the boat is Dutch registered,' we explained.

'But, you are British,' he observed.

Here we go again I thought as Peter asked why this seemed to be a problem.

'Not a problem,' Noel said. 'Unusual though.' He went on to explain that, in Belgium, it was more normal to fly the flag of the proprietor's nationality. We quite liked the sound of that. We thought it might be nice to fly the Red Ensign rather than the Dutch flag that was something of a red rag to a bull.

I was gratified that Noel noticed my tee shirt effort. He told us that it was very good to have the red and white flag. 'But,' he went on, 'it is not good that you do not have a Belgian courtesy flag.'

We felt duly chastened. We did know that etiquette said we should fly a courtesy flag of whichever country we sailed in. This was another flag we had been remiss about whilst stationary for months.

More firewood was collected in the morning. This time for a barbecue. I was preparing a salad and thinking how nice holidays are when I was disturbed by the sound of a substantial splash. Going on deck to see if Peter was still on board, I saw Noel swimming across the river. Peter leaned over the side and a dripping Noel, clutching a sock in one hand and a Belgian flag in the other, was hauled on deck. With a deep bow, Noel presented the flag with his compliments, then pulled a bottle of white wine out of the sock.

The flag was ceremoniously hoisted, and we drank a toast – well, a few toasts actually – to Belgium. It did seem a bit bizarre. Two Brits and a French man, total strangers, sitting on a half converted Dutch cargo barge toasting Belgium in wine conveyed across the river in a sock!

Time to move on; we had only a few days left. Being Sunday, the blast furnace was dormant, and we passed through Charleroi untainted and turned into the Brussels Canal that would take us back to Kappelle op den Bos. We had overlooked the fact that, being Sunday, these locks were closed. Had we been aware of this, we could have spent another lovely day at the Noel and Nellie mooring. As it was, we were forced to stay overnight in the near vicinity of Charleroi.

The water was horribly black and dirty and choked with debris of the non biodegradable sort. I watched, fascinated, as a car drove up and stopped beside the canal. A man got out, opened the car boot and took out eight or nine plastic bags of rubbish. He threw the bags into the canal, got back into his car, and drove away. Presumably he lived in Charleroi. It's a grim place to live, and the man probably saw no reason not to pollute it further!

The Brussels locks seemed so much easier to negotiate than when we had passed through four weeks earlier. The lifting bridge lifted as we approached, and the controller waved from his tower. We were happy to see our nice mooring wall awaiting our return. A lock full of fast moving ships had to be dodged before we were able to pull alongside our wall, where the Dutch sand barge was already in temporary residence. The Dutch couple and the diminutive Belgian's wife came to take our ropes and call, 'Welcome back.'

We felt we had come home. After sharing a mooring up drink with the welcoming committee, I said to Peter, 'I do still like the Dutch.'

'And I do like living in Flemish Belgium,' he replied.

Chapter Eight

GROWING PAINS

We continued to live at Kapelle op den Bos for a further eighteen months, but we moved from the elephant's trunk. Always conscious of the twenty four hour rule, we had often looked longingly at a mooring close by which had several advantages. It was in an area off the main canal and out of the stream of the constant heavy traffic. Barges awaiting cargo rested there, and I felt I would be less nervous at night amongst other boats. Also, the spot we favoured was close to the lock which, being well lit at night, meant I would be happy to walk the shorter distance to the 'phone box if the need arose.

The mooring had one severe disadvantage – it was already occupied. A classy, expensively converted private barge languished at bollards that carried it's name. Nobody lived on board, and the owner visited only occasionally. A few times, the barge bow-thrusted it's way from the bank and mini cruised for an hour or two. I watched, hoping that its propeller would choke with weed, leaving it incapacitated before a lifting bridge that didn't lift so it couldn't return to its mooring. But, with bowthruster in overdrive viciously churning the water, the barge always returned. I always waved graciously and smiled hypocritically from my bobbing deck.

I have never envied anyone's jewellery, fur coat, big house or smart car – except perhaps a Lotus Elan – but I really coveted that fancy barge's mooring.

Shortly before we had left to go on our cruising holiday, the fancy barge had disappeared. On our return, we observed that the mooring it had occupied was still vacant, except for a small motor boat owned by our friend George. It was George who told us the classy barge would not be returning. He encouraged us to move across to behind his own boat. He also took Peter to the Canal Authorities Office and helped to arrange for permission to stay there.

A permit to stay indefinitely on the canal was subject to Belgian survey regulations. As this required a fairly expensive survey, we took the opportunity to re-register Colibri as a Belgian vessel. George contacted a local surveyor and all was arranged.

We filled up with water from the trunk and, happy in the knowledge that nobody would ask us to leave, we moved to our new site. That evening, after Peter left for work, I sat on the side deck and gloated. For the first time, with the well lit lock and phone box nearby, I wasn't nervous about being on board alone at night.

We were more than willing to keep an eye on George's boat in return for his invaluable assistance. I would have done so in return for the kitten anyway.

Pauline brought me the tiny scrap of orange and white fur in her handbag. In true Lady Bracknell style, I said, 'A handbag!' And I said that we must call him Ernest. Peter said that he thought Ernest was a silly name for a cat so we should call him Brian.

Brian was adorable, and I was delighted to have his company at night. He snuggled in bed with me, purring loudly enough for a cat twice his size. The parrots were kept cage bound for two days; during which time, we reprimanded Brian whenever he tried to climb on the cage. When we felt confident that the kitten had learned not to go to the parrots, we let the parrots out.

Dillon immediately climbed onto the top of the cage and called, 'Brian. Come on Brian.'

We had worried unnecessarily. It was immediately obvious that the parrots and kitten had a healthy respect for each other. Storm and Dillon accepted Brian sitting on top of their cage as long as he didn't poke paws into their territory. Likewise, Brian did not object to a bird sitting on each arm of his chair as long as they didn't peck him.

Ducks proved to be a greater hazard than parrots for a tiny kitten. Perched on the deck edge, watching me feed bread to some mallards, Brian's little mind must have decided that it would be nice to visit these ducks at closer quarters. He jumped into the canal. I didn't push him, he didn't fall – he jumped. I suppose, looking at it through an immature cat's eyes, it must have seemed as if the ducks were walking on a firm surface. Of course, it must surely be prudent for a kitten, destined to spend life on a boat, to learn to swim early in that life. Protesting vociferously, Brian swam the length of the barge, round the bow and climbed up the bank before I had a chance to locate and grab a boat hook. Aware that I would probably have damaged, even drowned, the poor little devil with a useless boat hook anyway, Peter attached a potato net to a wire coat hanger and fixed it to a pole for future reference.

With our holiday over, and Peter back at work, life went back to normal. I said this to my Mother in a letter. She wrote back: 'What exactly do you mean by normal, Dear?'

How *do* you define normal? I suppose it means what you usually do. What we usually did these days was build a home inside a cargo barge. Like any normal housewife, I made beds. The fact that I did so with a saw and a ratchet screwdriver is beside the point. Mind you, even I protested that laying several tons of concrete paving slabs wouldn't normally be expected of the average housewife.

Ballast is important to the manoeuvrability of a boat, was one of the gems of advice we received from the Leeuwarden shipyard. They were right of course, a cargo vessel is designed to carry a lot of weight. We saw enough barges gliding down the canal with water lapping over the side decks. It still amazes me that they don't sink! We had also seen how unhappy an empty barge is in a strong wind.

Colibri had some ballast, but not enough. Peter would have had more control at Dinant if Colibri had been heavier and not so high above water level. I remember asking the shipyard if we could simply order a load of readymix concrete and have it poured into the bottom of the boat. Guess what they said – 'You could do that, but . . .' Apparently, a lot of people did do that, but problems can occur if the bilge is sealed with solid concrete. We were advised to lay concrete slabs on top of the hold floor. Several reasons were given to support that advice: A hull should remain flexible, the bilge should remain open and slabs could be positioned where weight was needed in order to obtain a good balance. We were not prepared to argue with any of that.

The hold floor consisted of massive oak planks. They had been there a long time and carried a lot of weight over the years. With difficulty, we lifted a few floor planks and discovered that they were as solid as iron. More than capable of bearing the meagre weight of two or three layers of concrete paving slabs.

'But, are we capable of bearing the weight of two or three layers of concrete slabs?' I asked. 'After all, I am a mere woman.'

'Nonsense,' said Peter. 'You're a tough little lady.'

It never fails to amaze me that my husband expects me to be feminine and cuddly, but assumes that I can emulate a twenty stone hairy labourer when occasion demands.

Just for starters, four pallets of concrete slabs were ordered. Delivery at ten o'clock Thursday morning was promised. Thursday dawned grey and pouring with rain. I pulled bed covers over my head and wondered if, by any chance, delivery of our slabs would be late – as in a day or two late.

Little chance. One of the nice things about Belgium is, that if someone says they will deliver something at a certain time, you can rely on being able to gloat over your something by ten past that certain time. I never had a washing machine repaired in Belgium, but I don't doubt that, if a repair engineer said he would come at ten next day, I would be out shopping at eleven whilst my washing swirled in a repaired machine.

Those slabs would arrive, and we would have to cope with loading them in wet weather. I emerged from my covers and peeped at the bedside clock. Ten past eight, I could snuggle down for another twenty minutes at least.

Peter got up and went to the loo. A crash, a vehemently ejected human oath and a sharply executed feline screech intruding into my sleepy state ruled out the possibility of even feigned sleep. A tentatively opened eye witnessed the spectacle of my husband's naked bum being ever so gingerly lowered onto the edge of the bed. Knowing full well that I really didn't want to hear the answer, I asked what was wrong.

'You're not going to believe this,' came the reply. 'The damn cat has just put my back out.'

'You're right – I don't believe this! How many concrete slabs did you order?'

'Four pallets.'

'Great! How many slabs is that?'

'Not sure exactly how many – about two and a half tons.'

'So, I'm going to have to lift two and a half tons on my own?'

'Not exactly. There's about two and a half tons to each pallet. That makes . . .'

'I know what four times two and a half make! Are you up to putting the kettle on?'

It rained all day. In fact, it positively bucketed down. And ten tons of wet concrete is heavier than ten tons of dry concrete – believe me, I know. At the end of the day I collapsed into a chair. Peter leaned over me at a funny angle and tenderly wiped grey grit off my chin.

'Well done, my love. I'm so proud of you.'

A tear of emotion, strongly mixed with exhaustion, made a grey rivulet down my cheek. As this was being even more tenderly wiped with a piece of kitchen roll, I gazed into my husband's eyes and asked, 'Why the . . . am I doing this?'

'Because, my love . . .'

'If you dare to tell me there are three sides to a concrete slab, I'll hit you!'

'No you won't, you haven't got the strength left.'

We walked around with a starboard list for ten days. Ten tons of concrete stayed where I had stacked it – at the nearest point to the front door – whilst Peter and I both recovered. Then it was only a simple case of redistributing the slabs in layers all over the hold floor. It actually required several more pallet loads to satisfactorily ballast Colibri to a sensible depth. Some areas needed more weight than others. A split level lounge and dining room not only looked rather nice, but achieved a good trim, enabling the boat to sit level in the water. That is, provided that the fresh water tanks on the port side and the diesel tanks on the starboard side are equally full or empty. Otherwise, a slight uphill trend one way or the other adds variety to our lives.

We carefully adjusted the content of the two tanks before laying the concrete base for the fireplace. It was essential to have the boat as level as possible whilst a five inch deep bed of wet cement hardened. Five and a half inches tapering to four and a half inches would mean forever living with an askew cast iron stove. I had visions of huge pots of winter warming soup keeping hot on top of the stove. I was not happy with a sudden flashing vision of Peter on his knees, spooning soup off the floor after a huge pot had slowly eased it's way down an inclining stove top.

The bed of cement took several days to set, but it looked level enough. The fact that Brian walked across it when it was still soft, his little paw prints forever cast in stone added an attractive aspect. I signed Brian's name below the paw prints, and it seemed a shame when we covered them with quarry tiles.

If the little darling had climbed the rubber plant and broken the leaves off before the cement had set, there may have been more than paw prints and a name embedded in concrete.

Now Peter can turn his hand to most things. As an avionics engineer, he's a pretty good plumber, carpenter, electrician, glazier, lumberjack etc.

He's a lousy bricklayer.

After watching him make a hash of three layers of a brick fireplace, I decided to take over. I had carefully hand picked expensive old Brugge Rose bricks. The ones Peter laid were so covered in sloppy grey cement that they may just as well have been cheap fletons. Okay, so I'm not a master bricklayer either, but even Peter acknowledged that my efforts did at least look like brickwork.

A visiting friend, who just happened to be a Belgian bricklayer, caught me at this activity and expressed clucking disapproval. Whether it was at me scooping up cement and spreading it with my hands, or at Peter sitting watching his wife carry out manual work, I'm not sure. Such was Nikale's concern that, bless him, he turned up next day, tool bag in hand, and took on the task of building us a fireplace.

I joined Peter in the spectators' gallery and watched row after row of expensive Brugge Rose evolve into a fireplace before my very eyes. Those very eyes told me that my fireplace sloped, ever so slightly, and leaned to port. Peter agreed that his eyes told him the same story. Nikale's spirit level told him all was well. We didn't want to offend our friend, but I worried that the perfectly perpendicular soup pot of my dreams would look silly against a sloping fireplace. Aware that this unbalanced scene could, given time, unbalance my mind, I opted to tell a professional bricklayer that his bricks leaned.

We diplomatically explained that the water tanks were half

empty, but the diesel tank was full. In order to demonstrate the problem of changing levels, we asked Nikale to watch the spirit level while we walked from one side of the boat to the other. The bubble in Nikale's spirit level followed us.

Accepting that a spirit level is not valid on a boat, Nikale produced a plumb line from his bag. A repeat performance by us convinced Nikale that a plumb line is equally invalid on a boat, for exactly the same reason. A bemused Belgian bricklayer asked how he was to tell if his bricks were leaning one way or the other.

'We know the concrete base is level,' Peter explained. 'We must now see if the bricks are square to the base.'

'Yes, that is good.' Nikale, scratched the inevitable flesh above a bricklayer's belt. 'How?'

Producing a metal square from his tool kit, Peter placed it on the concrete base and against the brickwork. It was discovered that the wall did lean slightly to port, and this was easily rectified with a series of trowel tapping

Nikale was impressed with this magic square thing. He declared that, in future, he would always use this good English tool. And he would tell all his work mates about it.

So, if you ever pass through Belgium and see a house on a hillside which is at perfect right angles to the land – betcha Nik the Brick and his mates built it.

My eighty year old mother had a loveable eighty two year old neighbour called Ernie. Ernie seemed fascinated by the fact that I lived in Belgium. Eventually, the root of his interest came to light. He had been twelve years old when he last saw his Father. His Father had been killed in Flanders in 1917.

It occurred to Ernie that, as I was in Belgium, I may be able to find out where his Father's grave was. All he knew was that it would probably be somewhere around Ypres. A difficult task this. Of the thousands of British soldiers killed in Flanders in the First World War, where to start looking for the grave of one of those men! But, this particular "one of those men" was Ernie's Dad. We felt compelled to find out something – anything. We had to at least try.

Annie, a Belgian friend, worked for a newspaper in Brussels. I thought she would have some idea where we could begin our search. Annie had no idea, but she asked questions at work. Suggestions were made and one thing led to another. After a series of 'phone calls, Annie was directed to the Commonwealth War Graves Commission. A call to them revealed the name of the cemetery, the row number and the grave number of Corporal Hardwicke of Ipswich.

Thoroughly caught up in the spirit of the investigation, Annie offered to drive us to Ypres. We complied gladly; there was no way we could exclude Annie from this bit. She took us to Brandhoek Cemetery number two, and I believe she was as thrilled as we were to discover Ernie's Dad's grave. I took a complete film of shots of the cemetery, the headstone, the row of headstones and the entry in the Commemorative book.

On our return to Kapelle, I took the film to be processed. Two days later, I collected blank negatives and the shop's apologies. It wasn't their fault, my camera had malfunctioned. Not one single print was available. Annie was so disappointed that she drove me the eighty miles back to Ypres the following weekend. This time she took her own camera, and refused to allow me to pay her for the excellent set of photographs she produced. 'A gift for your Mother's friend,' she insisted.

The name on the headstone was clearly shown, as was the entry in the book which said: Corporal William Hardwicke, Royal Medical Corps, Aged 40, Son of J. Hardwicke, Ipswich, Suffolk.

I wrote to Ernie and told him how our Belgian friend had, first discovered the whereabouts of the grave, then taken us to the cemetery. He took the letter next door to my Mother. He said nothing; just put the letter in Mother's hand and sat down and cried. I met a similar reaction when I took the photographs to Ernie. He clutched my hand, too emotional to speak. He was so moved by this positive evidence of his Father, and extremely touched by the fact that a totally unknown Belgian lady had gone to so much trouble to do this for him.

I was very moved by my visit to the war cemetery in Ypres. It was beautifully kept; with flower beds and neatly cut grass. The visitors book showed evidence of many recent visitors from Britain and elsewhere. The comments column was full of entries like: "Well done our lads" and "Bless you, we will always be proud of you". Feeling inadequate to add to those sentiments, I simply wrote: Thank you, Belgium, for honouring our men in this way.'

We had been to the point of Japanese surrender on the Malaysian island of Labuan, walked on the Bridge over the River Quai and visited war cemeteries in Malaysia and Thailand, but if it hadn't been for Ernie's Dad, we may well have neglected to look at what was on our doorstep in Flanders.

Did you know that, to this day, the traffic stops in Ypres at eight o'clock every evening and a lone trumpeter plays The Last Post?

The longer we stayed in Belgium, the more our fondness for the Flemish people grew. Considering that they were originally agricultural workers, and less educated than the Walloons, it surprised us how many Flemings spoke English and French in addition to their own language. Whereas, the one time considered upper class and better educated Walloons seemed to speak only French. Belgium is not much bigger than East Anglia, but they have a king. When the King of Belgium gives a speech to the Nation, he does so in three languages – a small group of his subjects on the border near Aachen being German speaking. Just imagine a king of East Anglia having to deliver a speech in Suffolk dialect, Norfolk dialect and whatever it is they speak in Peterborough!

I was told that English wasn't taught in Flemish schools until a couple of generations ago. Many older people have learned English by watching television, which explains why they often speak it with an American accent! Admittedly, it's not always good English that is spoken. All things, be they people or inaniamate objects, are often referred to as she.

'She said the weather get's better tomorrow,' the lady in the timber yard informed me. I assumed the weather forecaster was a woman, but George told me it wasn't. 'She don't does have women to tell the weather,' he said. The "she" in this case being the television.

And that was another thing. Negatives tend to be expressed as 'don't'. For example, George would tell us, "You don't must do that" or "I don't can remember". Of course, the latter does neatly dispose of the need to use the past tense. All clever stuff to someone like me, who struggles with anyone else's language and, more often than not, relies on someone else to use mine.

The arrival of Autumn turned our attention to the fact that our poor generator couldn't possibly be asked to carry responsibility for another winter. It had slogged it's little guts out and was overdue for retirement. A considerable number of lights had been installed with progressive ceiling placement, and we were now asking a lot of our existing batteries. We needed bigger battery capacity and a sensible generator to feed them.

Thoughts turned back to the shipyard at Leeuwarden. They had been so helpful, and had offered future assistance if needed. It was needed. Peter 'phoned to ask their advice on where to obtain a suitable generator. Their knowledge enabled them to estimate our current and our future requirements, and they could obtain a suitable generator at a good price. All we had to do was collect it from Leeuwarden.

A Monday in October saw us driving back to Friesland. There and back in one day was possible, but tiring. The shipyard boss booked us into an hotel that he considered to be inexpensive but good. It was rather comforting to be back in his hands, he still seemed to know our needs better than we did.

On arrival, we were shown our new generator. It was a lot bigger than I had expected, and it weighed about three quarters of a ton. No problem, a crane and men were standing by to load it into the jeep tomorrow. Meanwhile, we had a meal, then reported in to the arranged hotel.

The hotel's facade was fairly average, but the lobby led into a lounge and bar area that had an air of genteel opulence. A heavy chandelier, old but quality carpets and an abundance of decorous hardwood caused me to whisper, 'It doesn't look inexpensive.'

'Oh well,' said Peter, 'The generator cost less than I expected; we can afford this.'

When we went upstairs to our room, it seemed like we were entering a different hotel. From an ornate banistered, five star carpeted stairway, we progressed through three levels of diminishing grandeur. Carpets decreased in thickness as stars fell behind us. Our room was spartan, but clean and functional.

The heating, on the other hand, was six star, and the shower had the dimensions of a rugby club changing room, with sufficient scalding hot water for the grubbiest rugby team. The shipyard boss did indeed know the requirements of two people in the throes of converting a barge. The warmth and unlimited supply of hot water were heady stuff. We showered twice on our own and once together. Like deprived kids at the seaside on a sunny day, we revelled in this sheer luxury. The bill we paid in the morning can hardly have covered the cost of the hot water we used, not to mention the heat we were forced to let out of the window because we couldn't turn the radiator down.

It took four men, a crane and a forklift truck to load our generator into the jeep. I was detailed to watch the front wheels to see if they lifted off the ground. Having satisfied themselves that we were in a safe enough condition to drive back to Belgium, the shipyard crew waved and smiled as we drove away.

On the drive home, it occurred to us that the smiles could have been engendered by their anticipation of the ensuing pantomime – one man and his wife unloading what it had taken four men, a crane and a forklift truck to load!

Peter drove to work that night with the lump of machinery still in the back of the jeep. He enlisted volunteers to visit at the weekend to deal with the problem of getting one generator out of one jeep onto one barge. I assumed that Peter would drive the thing backwards and forwards to work until the weekend. Not at all, he was confident that he and I could get it out onto the canal bank. Piece of cake really – it only took a few minutes and most of my finger nails to slide the lump out of the jeep and onto a pile of carefully placed pallets. There it sat on the bank, awaiting a team of aircraft engineers to get it up onto the deck and down into the engine room. Heaven alone knew how!

Peter was asleep Thursday morning when a lock operation reduced the canal water to a level that really excited me. The generator, on it's platform of pallets, was exactly level with Colibri's roof. Surely, with a substantial plank to bridge the gap between land and roof, we could slide the generator onto the barge.

Peter was disgruntled at being woken after only three hours sleep. He wanted to know why I was telling him to come and look at the water level.

'Ahah! I see what you mean,' he said, his gruntle becoming

instantly less dis.

Ships were approaching the open lock. We figured that we had maybe thirty minutes before a locking changed the water level again. Dare we risk being stuck with three quarters of a ton of machinery mid plank between land and roof?

'Go for it,' said Peter. We went for it.

Inch by inch, we cautiously eased the genny along a plank and onto a pre placed square of old carpet on the roof. The carpet made it easier to slide the weight as well as protecting the paintwork.

'If we slid the carpet down the deck, we could get it just that bit closer to the engine room,' Peter suggested.

I shot him a look of utter disbelief. My shoulders and arms already felt as if they had been subjected to a particularly vicious assault course, and here was Peter asking for more! I mean, was this or was this not damned unreasonable? Gingerly flexing my sore bits, I pondered this question. I had yanked Peter out of bed to do this after a nights work and only three hours sleep. No, I didn't think he was being unreasonable. I might hate him, but he wasn't being unreasonable.

I checked that I still had eight fingers and said, 'Okay, encore.' I did wonder if we couldn't have backed the jeep and landed the genny closer to the engine room, but this wasn't the time to ask dumb questions.

'Of course, we could have roped the boat forwards and positioned the engine room beside the pallets,' said Peter, thirty agonising minutes later.

Thanks Peter!

We now had the genny at the aft edge of the roof. All that remained was a two foot level difference between roof and deck, then a seven foot drop onto the engine room floor.

'Don't even think it!' I said, backing off into femininity. 'I've already done far more than any sane woman of my age would even contemplate!'

'Block and tackle,' said Fernand, the diminutive Belgian, peering into the depths of the engine room. 'I've got some on my barge.'

I hugely admired the achievement after the event, but during it, I was too scared to watch Peter and a man smaller than me lower three quarters of a ton of machinery swinging on chains and pulleys. In fact, I seem to remember stomping off in disgust, throwing stuff over my shoulder like: 'If you two idiots are determined to kill yourselves, count me out as an audience!'

You wouldn't believe how a six kilowatt generator can affect a person's life! Electric heaters were bliss and I was promised a washing machine for Christmas. I was ecstatic at the thought of liberation from those loathed hours in public laundrettes. Things like hairdryers and irons re-entered my life. That novelty didn't last long, my hair had been happily drying naturally for nearly a year, and I scorched the first blouse I ironed. I heard Peter comment, 'Give her a hammer drill and she's okay. Put a domestic iron in her hand and she goes to pieces.'

The Black and Decker staple gun loved all this new power. With uninhibited exuberance, it thumped staples clean through wooden boards and out the other side. We reduced the thump setting and gleefully went back to all enveloping clothing, chiffon scarves and baby oil. The balaclavas I'd knitted instead of wasting wide awake time on my own at night was a case of bobble hats eat your heart out.

The two smaller bedrooms were ceilinged in a week. The kitchen area received the same crowning glory in time for the arrival of the washing machine. A gleaming, full sized gas cooker was also installed in time to cook Christmas dinner. Of course, lifting these two appliances out of the jeep, along the side deck, down the front steps and into the kitchen was a mere stroll in the park for people who had cut their teeth on concrete slabs and generators.

The new batteries were incredibly heavy, but we managed to man and womanhandle them on board. We went around flicking switches and saying really trite things like: 'Let there be light.' To think, there once was a time when I took all these things for granted – would you believe that?

Our optimism of Spring had been well founded. Colibri was indeed evolving into a civilized, comfortable home. We still had a long way to go, but the worst was behind us. Already, we were wondering how we had managed to cope with the previous winter.

The much longed for cast iron wood burning stove was ordered. The man from the shop came to see where it was to be installed.

'It maybe weighs a quarter of a ton,' he said, doubtfully looking at the passage from land to the fireplace. 'But, it can be taken apart and carried in sections,' he suggested more cheerfully.

'Nothing to it,' I declared. 'I could almost do it myself.'

When the man delivered the stove, he brought his mother and father, his wife and two children to see the boat where the stove was to live. When I went to the shop a week later to buy a big soup pot, I was greeted like a family friend.

The anniversary of the week we took up residence on board, Peter took a week off work for the event of our moving out of the aft quarters and into the part built main quarters. Two directors chairs were placed on a six foot by six foot square of carpet in front of the fire; a cosy little oasis in a sea of grey concrete. The fire was ceremoniously lit with the sticks I had collected at the Noel and Nellie mooring in summer. Using a slice of tree trunk as a table, we ate our first meal in our new lounge, washed down with some bubbly French stuff some people on a hire boat had given us. After the meal, we moved the carpet oasis into the far corner of the room away from the intense heat of the fire.

So impressed were we by the superb efficiency of the cast iron wood burner that I
went searching for a smaller one for the aft quarters. Made in Taiwan, the stove I found stood on four flared legs. Each side was heavily decorated with a scene of a man singing
a full chested aria to a full chested woman whilst gesturing dramatically to a range of mountains. This presumably depicted a scene from a Taiwanese opera, but suggested an amateur drama group's attempt at The Sound of Music where the set builder has gone over the top.

We gave the little diesel heater to Fernand. I don't know why we did that; we really liked Fernand a lot.

With the weight of so much heavy equipment added in various parts of the boat, a reshuffle of ballast was called for. Thank you Lex and your merry men up there in Friesland. Were they right, or were they right to tell us that concrete slabs were ideal versatile ballast?

With Christmas approaching, we were to attend a Company

function. Whoopee! A chance to dress up as a woman! I resurrected a skirt, bought some tights, and bathed in essence of white spirit.

Peter introduced me to one of the Company's Belgian security guards – a petite, pretty little girl in her early twenties. 'Are you a friend of Peter?' she asked.

'I hope so,' I replied, 'I'm his wife.'

'But you can't be! You don't look like his wife.'

Flashing a sweet smile at my husband that said: 'So, you work all night do you? And you don't tell me how pretty the security guards are!' I asked the young lady what Peter's wife did look like. Her next words released the pressure of my high heel on my husband's foot.

'He talks about you a lot,' she told me. 'And about your barge. I just imagined you would look different.'

Intrigued, I asked how I was supposed to look.

'Well . . . like Peter,' she said.

'But a beard wouldn't suit me,' I pointed out.

By talking to this girl, I gained the impression that, because Peter had a beard, wore jeans and lived on a barge, she had assumed that his wife would have long tatty hair reaching down to paint smeared jeans over a sloppy sweater designed to conceal the hefty body that took lifting generators in it's stride. My beskirted eight stone, topped by neatly coiffured, de-varnished hair, had completely blown Peter's credibility.

On the drive home, I suggested to Peter that maybe it wasn't good for my image if tales of my everyday activities were related at work. Peter looked disappointed. He said that the men enjoyed hearing about my brick-laying and things.

I got my own back – I told Peter's work mates that he borrowed my chiffon scarf.

Our second Christmas on board was a damn sight more comfortable than our first. For starters, we had an oven in which to cook a turkey. I don't tell many people this, but I actually made some pastry and baked mince pies!

Peter was working the night of New Year's Eve. George and Pauline took me out for a meal with their son and his wife, and we greeted the New Year before I was delivered home. I assured my friends that I was fine on my own, but I lied. I wasn't fine, I was lonely and wishing Pete was here. Being of Scots descent, New Year is important to Peter, and I was saddened by his absence on this special night.

Even Brian had deserted me to go moonlight hunting. At one o'clock, I sighed and moved towards my lonely bed. Through the bedroom curtains, I saw car headlights flashing on the bank. A car door opened and a radio blared out the chimes of Big Ben.

'I made it in time!' yelled Peter as he banged on the sheet of ply wood that posed as our front door. 'Happy New Year!'

Greeting him with a huge hug and a similar sized tumbler of whisky, I pointed out that midnight had been an hour ago.

'Not in Britain,' he replied, as the car radio belted out Auld Lang Syne.

Together, we spent the first night of our second year on Colibri; enjoying the warmth and comfort of our first year's efforts.

Chapter Nine

PLANNING TO LEAVE HOME

I took photo's of Colibri covered in snow. I took photo's of her foredeck piled high with discs of tree trunks. When the weather was bright and frosty, I took delight in cutting and chopping firewood on the bank.

I had never been allowed to use my chain saw, but I was permitted to use Peter's special axe. He had treated himself to no ordinary axe; this was one of those stainless steel shafted, rubber handled jobs that cost three times as much as an ordinary axe.

Emerging from sleep one lunch time, Peter stood in the wheelhouse and watched me bow sawing some branches Brian and I had collected. From the nice neat pile of logs, I took a thick one and picked up the axe to split it. Brian jumped onto the neat pile and scattered the logs. Out of the corner of my eye, I saw a little log roll towards the canal. Quick as a flash, I dropped the axe and caught the wayward log just as it reached the edge of the bank – and just as Peter's precious axe bounced on it's rubber handle and leaped into the canal. I had saved the little log though! I looked up at Peter, expecting wrath and indignation. He was convulsed with giggles.

Sharing a drink with Peter and his fellow workers in the Zaventem bar the following week, I greeted a late comer.

'Hi, Meg,' responded the late comer. 'Drowned any good axes lately?'

I turned to the well built panel beater beside me and said, 'Would you hit my husband for me please? You're stronger than I am.'

The battle of the wall boards didn't end in divorce because neither of us could cope with the prospect of a custody battle over Colibri.

We were jubilant when the last piece of ceiling was placed. It was a milestone ticked off; a job completed. We were left with a whole pack of four inch wide pine ceiling boards, and we thought they would solve the problem of the curved upper wall in the lounge. The main walls were clad in marine ply, but it was proving difficult to bend thick plywood round this fairly acute curve above side deck level. Vertically placed pine boards would sort of tie in with the pine ceiling, and should, in theory, look rather nice. The theory was fine whilst the wall was vertical. When it reached the curved bit, the boards began to slope, and I began to complain.

'It looks wrong,' I stated. 'We'll have to fan the boards round the bend.'

'Don't be silly,' said Peter, 'that would look ridiculous!'

'Well, it looks ridiculous with a lean.'

'Not as bad as if they were fanned out. That creates an optical illusion.'

'I can't live with leaning walls!'

'Geometrically, it's correct.'

'I don't want to live geometrically, I want to live sanely!'

The argument went on for three days, during which time, building came to a halt. This was getting us nowhere. We shelved the wall board project, and shelved the kitchen cupboards instead. But the half clad curved wall didn't go away.

Adjudication arrived in the shape of three aircraft engineers. Armed with a crate of beer, they called, unsuspectingly, to have a drink with us. We waited until they had the second beer in their hands before hitting them. We hit them quite hard with: 'You guys have got to settle a divorce here.'

One of them agreed with Peter. One of them agreed with me. Four pairs of eyes riveted on the third man, looking for a casting vote. It would have taken a brave man to cast that vote. What we had, cowering behind a beer can, was a sensible man.

'Why don't you just put up plywood and wallpaper?'

'Coward!' I accused him.

'Dead right. You two only have to live together – I have to work with Peter.'

Which instantly told me that he was really on my side.

Peter didn't agree.

In the end, instead of trying to force thick ply round the bend, we put three layers of fine ply. It looks very nice wall papered.

Returning home one dark evening, we were surprised to find we had a neighbour. A large converted barge was tied up alongside

Colibri. We guessed it had arrived in the dark and taken a convenient mooring for the night.

But the barge didn't move next day. In fact, there was no one on board.

'I recognise that boat,' Peter said, 'It's the same barge that was here before.'

'Don't be silly,' I replied scathingly. 'It's a totally different colour and has a different name! How can it be the same boat?'

'It's the same boat,' Peter insisted.

The owner – yes, it was the man from the classy boat whose mooring I had so coveted – had returned with a heavily disguised same boat to reclaim his mooring.

Apparently he had friends in high places. So? *We* had a piece of paper that said we had official permission to be there. We paid all of the equivalent of five pounds a month for this privilege, but the amount wasn't important. We were on the computer, and that's really important. No one challenges the computer.

It was amicably agreed that the barge would stay alongside us. The owner wanted his barge to be beside land, but we didn't want to have to climb over his barge to get to ours. Any animosity was quelled by the obvious ploy of pointing out that we were inbuilt security for an expensive unoccupied boat. Nobody could board his vessel without crossing Colibri first. He was not often on board, so him crossing Colibri was not a problem for us.

What was a problem, was that we were now trapped between a barge and land; meaning we couldn't easily get out to go and fetch water from the trunk. The solution was five gallon plastic jerry cans. Peter filled four of these each day at work, and this was sufficient for our needs. On frozen nights, Peter put hot water in the cans and loaded them into the jeep at six thirty in the morning. When everyone left work at seven, Peter was the only one to make an instant getaway whilst everyone else was still scraping ice from windscreens and longing for spring.

Before spring did arrive, a further toilet was installed; this time, in the first of two guest cabins. We didn't bother with the arms between legs bit; we boringly relied on measurements taken from the first round of the loo positioning saga. Positioning the hand basin outlet pipe offered potential entertainment though. It involved Peter hanging by his toenails to the deck while leaning over the side to screw a pipe fitting to the hull. I don't mind watching a man fall in water, it's only seeing them crushed under lumps of heavy stuff that I'm squeamish about. However, Peter's toes looked like hanging in there with grim tenacity, so I lost interest and wandered off to make a lemon meringue pie. I was wrist deep in flour when Peter called for some bread.

Bread! What on earth did the staff of life have to do with toilet outlets? Dripping flour and marge, I went up to ask – rather facetiously, I admit – if uncooked pastry would do.

'No,' came the muffled reply from an upside down man with his head at water level. 'I need you to decoy this damn swan with bread. It keeps pecking my hand!'

As usual, we greeted Spring and Summer with the joy and enthusiasm those delightful seasons accept as their God given right. But there would be no Summer cruising for us this year. As a contractor, Peter would forfeit pay by taking leave. Pay that had attained a high value because we planned to take the whole of next year off without any. We were becoming impatient to investigate the life of freedom that all our hard work was aimed at.

Meanwhile, we worked on building and painting until a heatwave in July melted our energy and enthusiasm, and made it impossible to spread paint on metal decks that were behaving like over efficient radiators. Bargee wives put bed sheets over crew quarters windows and threw children into the canal to cool off. I waved Peter off to work on torpid evenings; complacent in the feeling of security afforded by other barges being around me at night.

It was from a deep, relaxed sleep that I woke at two a.m. to a strange noise. Sitting bolt upright in bed, I listened intently and tried to identify the noise. It was vaguely familiar; I had heard those plastic noises before – but not here, in Belgium.

Encouraged, no doubt, by the tropical sound of a fan whirring above my head, my mind was obviously playing tricks. Either that or I was dreaming. I was on a beach in Borneo, hearing a wind surfer being unpacked and erected. There is something unique about the sound of a fibre glass surf board thumping sand and plastic sails being unfolded.

Looking through the curtains, I saw . . . no, it couldn't be! A young lad from a commercial barge was unpacking a wind surfer, right beside my bedroom window, at two o'clock in the morning on a Belgian canal bank. He didn't even look embarrassed when he saw me watching.

It was difficult staying stationary through that hot summer while nursing the difficult decision to relinquish a good salary and go for freedom. Okay, we had made that move once before when we went off on Tiger Lily, and it does get easier the second time. Still difficult though. As it happened, just when we were getting cold feet about devoiding ourselves of an income before Colibri was even finished, the die was cast for us.

The Belgian Company Peter worked for decided to let its British contract workers go. Their decision made our decision ever so much easier to carry out. The choice of whether or not to go for a new contract elsewhere didn't seem to apply. Instead, our instinct to go for a year off was reinforced.

Colibri hosted a farewell barbecue before Peter's fellow contract workers went their separate ways. Some, no doubt, to places where the sun shines quite often, but we had a good evening first. It was considered a good move to keep some of the guys on board for what was left of the night. We had one spare bedroom equipped with beds, otherwise, it was a case of sun loungers in the lounge.

At about four o'clock in the morning, I insisted that Guy went to bed. I wasn't prepared to take responsibility for leaving him on the bank because the chances of him getting safely on board by himself were remote. Mike was already sunbedded in the lounge; grabbing some sleep before reporting for airport duty at five. Trying to hush Guy's giggles, we managed to get him on board, down the steps, and onto a sun bed. He was a big man, and it wasn't easy.

Still breathless, we fell into bed, only to be alerted to the sound of Guy moving around. Peter heard him go on deck, and shot after him while I waited for the splash of a big man hitting water. At least, I hoped he had chosen the water side and not the wall to bounce off.

I can't imagine how Mike slept through the commotion of Peter trying to hold six foot three of uncoordinated weight upright so

Guy could pee over the side without falling in. We managed to put him back to bed, then retired again ourselves. Within minutes, we were shooting out of bed to smother Guy with a pillow, still hoping not to disturb Mike. Guy's sunbed had collapsed, and he was having hysterics.

The only solution was to roll him onto the floor and fold the sun bed on top of him.

Arriving home from a shopping trip a few days later, we found our way into the boat barred by an ironing board, two plastic garden chairs and several other items, including a baby conifer in a plastic mug. One of the departing contractors had cleared his Zaventem apartment. A note pinned to the ironing board said:

Bin anything you don't want – except the tree, I grew it from seed – Luv, Adrian.

The baby tree was instantly named Adrian, and all four and a half inches popped into an optimistically large terracotta pot on deck.

An era had come to an end. Again, we felt that someone or something was directing us. It happened a few months earlier than we had planned, which left us short of a few month's salary, but it did allow us an extra fifty hours a week of Peter's time with which to prepare Colibri for a year of freedom.

Memories of a rapid dismantling of wheelhouse for a French tunnel persuaded us to use the extra time to lower the wheelhouse. Fernand, with his cutting and welding gear, agreed to assist.

We had established good terms with our neighbour, and we were reluctant to cover his barge with *grin-ding* dust – or expose it to risk of fire from a gas cutter. A few sparks could have done untold damage to the other barge's plastic awning and astra turf, so, before embarking on this project, we moved Colibri back to the long wall by the elephant's trunk.

This came as a bit of a shock to Brian. Up until then, he hadn't been aware that his home was likely to – or even could – move. It wasn't until we were about to remoor, that it occurred to me to wonder if we had even brought the cat with us. Peter assured me that we had. As soon as the engine started up, he'd seen a quivering feline streak shoot down below.

We found him under our bed, and when he was persuaded to

re-emerge, he went to the wheelhouse door on the port side; obviously rather desperate to dig up some soil and relieve his bladder of the fright he had received. Grabbing him before, in his haste, he shot off the boat into the canal, I placed him on the starboard side deck. He stared at the land, which he knew damn well had never been on that side before, and looked up at me with a bemused expression on his face. When I picked him up and placed him on land, he stared around with sheer, *whatever has happened to my world?* amazement.

Trauma was almost instantly overcome by ecstasy as, spotting trees that hadn't been on his doorstep before, Brian sprinted to the nearest one and shot up into the branches. Taking just long enough out to use the field for the bodily function he had temporarily forgotten was desperate, he explored more trees, a hedge and a ditch; coming back to the boat at intervals to miaow and purr at us. He was either checking that we and his home were still there, or he was telling us all about his exciting new back garden.

We re-acquainted ourselves with a lady dog walker that we had been on waving terms with when we lived there before. On Friday, she waved at us as she headed for the leafy lane. We waved back from our intact wheelhouse.

Over the weekend, we took the wheelhouse roof and windows off and stacked them on deck under one of the faded brown tarpaulins that once graced Colibri's hatch covers. Peter and Fernand attacked the steel walls with angle grinders and gas cutters, reducing them by three feet. Burn scars from the gas cutter streaked what was left of the walls, and the hunks of cut off, burn scared metal were strewn on the bank.

Monday morning, with grave concern in her voice, the lady dog walker asked, 'What happened! Did she explode?'

Our friend, Annie, driving along the other side of the canal, nearly crashed her car in her haste to get to the next bridge so she could cross over to come and see if we were still alive.

This amused Fernand less than it did us. At one stage, when he was welding in the engine room below the wheelhouse, Fernand had succeeded in creating a small fire. Although small, it was potentially lethal in that it was uncomfortably close to the bank of batteries. Fernand admitted to closing his eyes and muttering, "Dear God, if you love me, please don't let those batteries explode", before yelling for mortal help.

'Stand aside!' commanded Peter, brandishing a bright red fire extinguisher.

An out of date fire extinguisher makes a noise not unlike that of a damp fart.

For most of the ten days it took for the wheelhouse to be lowered and extended forward, it poured with rain. The second faded brown tarpaulin was erected over the work area.

'It's like a Bedouin tent,' was Fernand's comment. 'It changes shape every day!'

It was okay for him, he could stand up beneath it, whereas Peter, being six foot tall, had to prop up the makeshift canopy according to whichever area he was working in.

I took coffee down the side deck to the labour camp, keeping most of the rain out by shielding the cups with a bag of doughnuts. Lifting the canvas, I found Peter on his knees, welding the new, further forward, front wall.

'Are you planning to drive the boat on your knees?' I asked.

'We're planning to lower the floor,' I was curtly told. This was good news, because the wheel was currently propping up the tarpaulin.

'How?' was my next inappropriate question. 'I mean, the floor is solid steel, and it's welded to the walls. Then there's the wheel and all that steering gear!'

They admitted that they hadn't actually, as in fully, worked out exactly how. It was time for a technical meeting over coffee and soggy doughnuts under a soggy, sagging Bedouin tent. Fernand's block and tackle was high on the agenda, as was the question of where to stand whilst cutting out the floor – on it or under it? Once again, I left them to it, and admired the results afterwards.

The result I most admired was a doorway from the new, bigger wheelhouse into our bedroom. Just think, if we had still been living aft, we could have gone to bed without going outside. But then, if we'd still been living aft, I would have become entombed in a bomb site replica, because the entrance to the aft quarters disappeared in the scheme of things. We didn't actually have access to the aft quarters again until a new lower entrance was cut – after the floor was lowered.

I was pleased when that happened because we needed to get

into the aft quarters to pinch a door. The wonderful new doorway to our bedroom had left us exposed to gales howling through the exra length of wheelhouse where no windows resided. One of four original teak, stained glass panelled doors had to be commandered to shield us from the elements as we slept.

A friend of Fernand, another would be converted barge owner, was impressed with the end product. 'Did you have the plans drawn professionally?' he asked.

'Plans!' spluttered Fernand. 'They are in his head – and he only lets them out a bit at a time.'

All the original teak framed windows were re-usable, but we now needed to fill two five foot gaps with additional windows. Out of deference to the fact that Peter was heavily engaged in re-connecting the lowered steering gear and re-siting the wheelhouse floor, whilst winter was forcing it's presence through two five foot gaps, a local woodworker was called upon to make new windows.

'The gaps are too small!' I wailed, when we offered up the smart new windows.

'No,' Peter patiently pointed out, 'the windows are too big.'

We passed this information on to Pieter the woodworker. He asked what exact size our gaps were. 'The windows are too big,' he agreed.

He also agreed to rectify this as soon as possible. As soon as possible, transpired into seven weeks. Apparently, dozens of Kappelle op den Bos owner occupiers had decided that rotting doors and windows, ignored all summer, must be attended to immediately winter showed it's face. Such was Pieter's chagrin at making the mistake in the first place, then keeping us waiting so long for it to be put right, that he insisted on giving Peter some spare timber as recompense.

'Just a little gift,' said Pieter. 'I don't want you to leave Belgium with bad thoughts of me.'

The spare timber was a heap of three inch by eight inch maranti hardwood planks. Each plank was in excess of eleven feet long and took two people to lift. Two people, namely, Peter and Pieter, lifted planks onto the jeep roof rack until, with a gasp of protest, the jeep's bulky tyres sank in despair. Two people, namely, Peter and Meg, unloaded six wonderful planks of beautiful hardwood onto Colibri.

'I can't believe he really gave you this much!' I said.

'He didn't. He gave me ten planks, but I left the rest behind because we couldn't get them onto the jeep.'

We left Belgium with very kindly thoughts of Pieter the Plank. We left Belgium with fond thoughts of many people.

Let's face it, we left Belgium with tears in our eyes.

Chapter Ten

A ROPE, A LADDER AND FREEDOM

Whilst we were deliberating on whether to go in March, or wait till better weather next month – guess what? – we were asked to move.

It was done very nicely. A canal Authorities man visited and pointed out that we were, strictly speaking, only allowed twenty four hours at the commercial mooring wall. We were welcome to stay on the canal, but it was preferred that we move back to our mooring by the lock. The man suggested that we move in a few days, maybe a week's time.

'Thank you, but we will be leaving altogether next Thursday,' Peter told him.

'Will we?' I asked. 'Why next Thursday?'

'Your birthday seems as good a time as any to start our new adventure.'

'Well – yes, I suppose . . .' I was suddenly scared of leaving our safe haven. Maybe it would be nice to just wait a bit? I had been very happy beside the lock; maybe we should turn the boat around and go back to our legitimate mooring for a while?

'The boat is pointing towards France,' Peter pointed out. 'Wouldn't it be a bit silly to turn and face the opposite direction; towards Antwerp?'

That settled it – I definitely didn't want to think about Antwerp. So, it was decided that, when we moved, it would be towards France.

For my birthday, I had a lovely thick, soft, supple nylon mooring rope and an aluminium ladder. The latter item was to become my best friend. During our summer cruise of two years before, I had often jumped ashore and scrambled up banks to reach a bollard. Fine in summer, but muddy banks in March would be less fun. With a rope loop through the top step of my ladder, I could hook it onto one of Colibri's bollards and alight with style.

Some goodbyes, and we were free to travel – wherever and whenever the fancy took us. On the morning of my birthday, I slipped the ropes off the same monster bollards that we had been so happy to embrace on our arrival at Kappelle op den Bos more than two years ago. Colibri looked a very different boat, and we were different people as we set sail for France.

'Where abouts in France?' people had asked. Who knew? Just sort of France in general, was our plan.

As it happens, someone's birthday is not necessarily a good criterion on which to base travel plans. Mine wasn't actually as good a time as any. It snowed on us at Ronquierres and the River Sambre was in serious flood.

Lock entries were hazardous, with the strong downstream current behind forcing us forward when we wanted to slow down. How on earth would we be able to slow down and stop to moor up? I was anxious to know. I was told that we would have to turn the boat to face into the flow.

The conditions we found ourselves in can best be described as being similar to those of a ten ton truck with no brakes travelling down a hill at fifteen miles an hour. The only way to park that truck would be to turn it to face uphill and throw a rope round a lamp post before the truck slid backwards down the hill.

Another way to describe it would be to think of a recurring nightmare – the one where you're falling through space and you hope you wake up before you reach the ground!

We followed a sturdy, powerfully engined tug round a bend, and there, confronting us all, was a lock. The tug didn't make it! Reverse gear caused it to slew sideways and, instead of entering the lock, it crashed, full frontal, into the lock cut wall. As it bounced off the wall, an equally sturdy, powerfully muscled man threw a thumping great rope an impressive distance onto a land bollard, and the tug shuddered to a halt; facing back the way it had come.

Witnessing this had an unnerving effect. We were taking the bend at super speed, couldn't slow down, and Peter didn't much fancy our chances of entering the lock either. We couldn't possibly moor with the downstream current behind us, so Peter pushed on power, turned Colibri, and headed for a wall on the opposite side of the river.

We had not allowed for the weir beside the lock. We didn't even see the weir until we began to slide sideways, very rapidly, towards it. It took every vestige of power Colibri's hundred and twenty horse power engine could deliver to swing her bow into the current so Peter could drive her forward towards the wall.

It's amazing how panic can engender strength. We were both impressed by the distance I managed to throw my new birthday rope! In my haste to secure my end, I badly bruised my knuckles, but I felt no pain until, from swinging precariously on a rope that I was sure would snap, Colibri eventually landed with a thump alongside the wall.

We put a lot of ropes on several bollards, and I noticed Peter crossing his fingers. Mine were swelling alarmingly by then, so I forwent the superstious bit and just hoped we would be safe for the night. We didn't even want to think about how the hell we were going to get off that wall tomorrow.

Tomorrow became today. I stubbornly insisted on washing last night's dishes before we left. This was not me being a diligent house keeper – this was me being shit scared. I wanted to delay the time when we took all those ropes off; knowing that, when we did, we must go for the lock we had bottled yesterday.

With my good hand, I stood flicking congealed grease across the surface of the cold washing up water, wondering if we could perhaps just stay where we were – or even return to Kappelle. We were facing that way now.

Peter had already called twice to ask if I had finished washing up. I knew I wouldn't get away with a third, 'Not yet.' I didn't even get that third chance to lie. The engine lurched into life, my stomach lurched in rebellion, and I threw up into the greasy washing up water.

Making my way up to the wheelhouse, I could see that the tug had gone. But which way? Did it turn and go through the lock, or did it give in and go home?

I wanted to go home!

Leaving a rope on until the last minute, with plenty of engine thrashing and no small amount of trepidation, we left the wall. My other apprehension was unfounded, based as it was on our high speed lock approach of yesterday. Then, we had skidded round a bend with gathering momentum; almost out of control with the current behind us. Today, we started from standstill, turned and edged our way round the wall that separated the lock from the weir. At a sedate and controlled speed, we entered the lock and passed through.

Once that hurdle was behind us, we became aware of the fact that we were hungry. We moored to a much longer, flow reducing wall on the approach to the next lock, and fed breakfast to stomachs that were now in a receptive mood. Eating on deck in sunshine, we watched literally hundreds of rabbits romp and frolic on the grassy spit of land that, comfortingly, separated us from another thrashing weir.

Anxious to vacate the River Sambre and face into the current of the River Meuse, we had hoped to make Namur that evening. However, due to my lengthy washing up exercise and our leisurely breakfast break, with one lock to go, we ran out of daylight and lock opening hours. As the sky was darkening with rain clouds and impending nightfall, I suddenly recognised where we were. Just ahead, was the lovely little wall where we had met Noel and Nellie.

Noel would not have splashed so nonchalantly across with his sock of wine in these conditions! The current was pushing hard from behind, but the canal was not wide enough to turn and head into the flow. We would have to make a downstream mooring. I would have to be damn quick with my rope. I knew the wall was short and that there were just three bollards.

I missed the first one. Rain in my eyes and an overhanging branch prevented me from seeing the next one, but I knew it was there somewhere. And I knew there were only two chances left. I spied bollard number two as the overhanging branch threatened to decapitate me. I had the choice between losing my face or losing the bollard. My face won that toss, but my next toss won the third and final bollard. Once again, we were safely moored for the night.

Peter bathed my scratched face while I picked twigs out of my rain sodden hair. My bruised knuckles were now introverted dimples, and my fingers resembled a half pound of swollen decaying sausages.

'Things will get easier when we start travelling upstream,' Peter promised.

'I believe you,' I said. 'But if I live to see my next birthday, could you please just buy me flowers and take me out to dinner?'

We woke to a bright, sunny day at the fondly remembered Noel and Nellie mooring. A couple of hours cruising would see us at

Namur. The plan was to stay in that pleasant town for a few days. We needed to shop for fresh supplies and to recharge our energy cells. Meanwhile, we had time to spend a while allowing Brian some freedom ashore in sunshine. He loved it here; he romped through the *bus-shes*, and we wandered through the woods collecting sticks in a potato net. This time, for our first lighting of the operatic aft fire.

Poor Brian had been somewhat bemused by this travelling business. His hitherto unharried life of six months had been spent in two places that were at least semi permanent homes. Now when we moored up each night and called Brian to come and see where he was, it was often on the opposite side to where we had been the night before. He would go to the door that had previously offered access to land, only to find an expanse of water confronting him. I knew the feeling well; first thing in the morning, I was prone to opening the door on the wrong side.

The Namur bollards that I had so nonchalantly roped on our summer cruise were lapped by high water now. Even if we had been able to stop there, it would have been a case of floating ropes. In a sideways skid, we made the turn out of the treacherous downstream flow of the Sambre, into the uphill battle against the much bigger Meuse, and came to an almost virtual standstill.

It was very definitely going to be easier to moor. I stood on the foredeck with a rope, looking at a bollard that, with four knots of current against us, we approached so slowly that I considered nipping below to peel some potatoes for dinner.

So far, we had given Brian nice country overnight lodgings where he could mooch around happily. He hated Namur; a town mooring with traffic roaring past and people walking by the boat. After two days, during which Brian had not been persuaded to disembark, we were becoming anxious about his bladder. We searched the boat to discover where he was relieving himself, but found no evidence that he was. Surely, we thought, the poor little sod hasn't had his legs crossed since we left the Noel and Nellie mooring!

It was when Peter announced that the bloody cat had dug up Adrian that I knew we had discovered Brian's outlet. Quite intelligently, I thought, Brian had adopted the plant pot as an emergency litter tray. We compassionately re-interred Adrian and, even more compassionately, sand filled an old washing up bowl and offered it to Brian as an emergency town toilet.

Three day's rest was all we were able to keep still for. We hadn't seen another boat moving in that time, but we felt both rested and restless, so intrepidly battled on.

The cliffs of the Ardennes looked even more dramatic under low slung heavy skies. It was slow work forcing our way up the flooded Meuse. It didn't get any easier when that river changed it's name to Canal de l'est at the same time as it changed from Belgian to French waters.

We left Belgium with refilled diesel tanks and ambivalent feelings. Excited to be on the threshold of our dreamed of exploration of France, we were, nevertheless, sad to be leaving the country that had been such an hospitable host for so long.

It seemed that even France had doubts about our desertion of Belgium. No one was in a hurry to let us in; it took ages for us to pass through the first French lock. We drove in, plopped a bollard and waited. Fifteen minutes later, we plopped another bollard and turned the engine off. Eventually, Peter went in search of someone prepared to act as a lock keeper.

The someone he found was digging his garden – and was most surprised to hear that there was a boat in his lock! He asked if we had seen any other boats; obviously wondering if he had time to plant his carrots before next week. We admitted that we hadn't actually seen any other moving boats for some days. 'C'est normale,' said the lock keeper, leaving us feeling that he considered us anything *but* normal. He locked us through then went back to his vegetable patch.

At the end of the lock cut, we were surprised to find a porte de garde closed to us. We definitely hadn't been expected today – didn't anyone here know about my birthday? We waited while a man took a box of bedding plants from the boot of his car and walked across the low bridge to his house. We waited while the man returned to his car and carried another box of plants across. The car boot yielded five boxes in total. When all were safely gathered in to the man's shed, he opened the porte de garde and let us through with a cheery wave. We wished him bon jardin.

Once again, we tried to report our presence in France. There was still no one at home to receive this information; important to us, but obviously of no particular interest to France. This indifference was a little deflating. We had waited a long time for this momentous entry into France. To mark the occasion, we declared to ourselves that Colibri had become a peniche, and continued on our way, confident that our peniche, with it's new low slung wheelhouse, would have no problem negotiating the first French tunnel without delay.

In the lock preceding the tunnel, the lock keeper eyed our wheelhouse doubtfully. Surely he didn't remember Colibri's wheelhouse being dismantled in his lock two years ago? He asked for the ship's papers and said, 'Ahah!' as a smile lit his face and his finger pointed to our given dimensions. In 'O' level French, Peter explained that we had physically altered the height, but had not transferred that detail to the meetbrief. We wondered if he was going to insist that we make the wheelhouse height conform with the printed details – or perhaps we would have to stay in the lock and wait until an official came to alter and stamp the details. However, he did operate the lock before telling us that we could not leave.

It was with relief that we realized we were only being detained while an Army officer in Action Man dress supervised a dozen soldiers swinging across the river on a wire. 'C'est normale?' asked Peter.

'Ah oui,' replied the lock keeper, picking up his hoe and returning to his cabbages, leaving us to exit his lock at such time as the bunch of pseudo Tarzans had completed their testicle freezing exercise.

At last, here was somebody to herald our arrival. Bowing to cheers and waves from a dripping and shivering French Army, we disappeared into the Ham Tunnel.

About where we thought the Charleyville Mezier lock should be, we came to double red lights on a bend. The lights stayed stubbornly red, so we tied to the light post, and Peter went off to interrupt another lock keeper's Percy Thrower activities.

This lock keeper was dozing in a bankside chair with a fishing rod on his lap. Peter was tempted to ask if he didn't have a vegetable patch to attend to, but asked, instead, why the lights didn't change to green. He received a reply on the lines of: Why should they when there are no boats around?

On hearing that a peniche was waiting, the man dropped his fishing rod and ran to the lock. Peter ran back to Colibri, but not before I had witnessed a change from red to green and wondered what the hell to do! We had waited twenty minutes for the green light. Would it change it's colour and it's mind before we could take advantage of it?

A breathless Peter leapt on board and motored round the bend. All I could see was another bend. Once round that, I saw what could possibly be a lock lurking over to one side at an acute angle away from the river. It actually called for a virtual U turn.

'I must admit,' Peter said, 'I'm glad I had to go on foot to find the lock keeper, otherwise I would never have known where to find his lock.'

Consuming considerably more diesel than our budget had strictly allowed for, we adjusted the budget and followed what we hoped was the main river course. Occasional trees or fence posts protruded from the river, indicating where the river's banks would normally be found. The water reached lower branches of trees, and fields either side accommodated a river three times it's usual width. It was quite beautiful, but a bit scary. And we really did seem to be out there on our own. We were quite excited when we sighted another boat coming towards us, and waved delightedly at evidence of not being alone in our madness as a small British flagged sailing boat called 'Smokey Joe' skated past with the downstream current up its tail.

We had promised to contact Son or Daughter weekly; one at weekends and one midweek. That way, we were not out of touch for more than three or four days, and one or other of the offspring knew roughly where we could be found should the need arise. It also gave us comfort knowing that someone in the real world had a vague idea where we were. This system worked provided we could find telephone boxes.

There would be telephone boxes at Sedan. We had planned to stop at Sedan. I'm not really sure why, except that we probably felt that we should. However, Sedan didn't hold much appeal. It seemed sort of municipal. This is difficult to explain because the place is so steeped in history. Maybe the municipality wanted to dislodge the grim image of a place known for defeat and multiple bloodshed from two centuries. A charming municipal marina is provided, which suggested that visiting boats were welcome, but I'm afraid we passed through and spent the night in a rural setting more to our taste.

Our chosen mooring for the weekend was delightfully green and tranquil, and the weather was warm and sunny enough to bring forth paintbrushes and industrious attempts to make the new wheelhouse look as if it belonged to the rest of the boat. But, there was no telephone box anywhere in sight, so I mounted the moped and went in search of a means to communicate with Daughter.

Sunday afternoon, the nearby village had no evidence of either a telephone box or any people who might even want one. I trundled around, looking at the village in which I was the only thing awake and moving. Even trees and bushes were motionless in the somnambulant atmosphere, and the only sound was the gentle purr of my moped's engine.

The two gendarmes materialized out of nowhere. One second the street was empty; next second, in perfect unison, one from the left and one from the right, the uniformed officials stepped into the street and planted themselves forbiddingly in my path. Screeching to an abrupt halt, I decided that, today, I could speak no French at all. I couldn't even manage bonjour.

'Good afternoon, gentlemen,' I said. 'I don't suppose, by any chance, either of you speak English?' My crossed fingers were to no avail. The younger gendarme could speak English – A leetle.

'Have you protection for your mobelette?' he asked.

Protection for my moped? What on earth did he mean? I looked my bike over for any obviously vulnerable parts that might, under French law, require protection.

'What do you mean by protection?' I asked.

'Protection, for your mobelette,' he repeated in a louder voice, which didn't help me at all. I wondered why, when people find you can't understand their language, they automatically assume you are also hard of hearing. I wanted to tell this man that I wasn't deaf, only English, but by then, I was beginning to wonder if he was talking about insurance. I was also wondering if we did have moped insurance that was valid in France. Stalling for time, I said: 'I'm very sorry, but I'm afraid I really don't understand what you mean.'

The young bilingual one spoke to the older monolingual one, who shrugged and tapped his head. This was okay by me; if they thought I was a nutty English woman, they would probably let me go rather than become involved with me.

The young one turned back to me and tapped his own head before pointing at mine. 'You must have the protection,' he stated.

'Oh! You mean for my head?' I grabbed at this possible let out.

'Certain for your head. In France, the hat crasher is law.'

'I didn't know that,' I explained. 'I've just arrived from Belgium, where the hat is not required by law.'

This, translated to the older one, seemed to give rise to some amusement. Both men looked at my little blue moped. Both men smirked. The older one pantomimed revving bike handles. Both men laughed loudly enough for even the deafest foreigner to understand their meaning.

Mustering the air of refined dignity that my British passport expects of me, I said, 'No, gentlemen, I do not ask you to believe that I came from Belgium on this little mobelette. Actually, I and my bike came by peniche.'

I didn't expect even the semi bilingual one to grasp all of that pompously delivered speech. What they did clutch on to was the word peniche. 'Ah!' said semi bilingual. 'Your peniche is called 'Colibri, oui? It is near the ecluse, oui?'

'Oui,' said I, forgetting that I was supposed to know no French.

So, they knew we were on their patch; had noted our presence and observed our Belgian flag – and I had learned that, in French, a lock is an ecluse.

It was carefully explained to me that, without a hat crasher, I must walk with my mobelette back to my peniche.

Peter was looking out for me, obviously wondering why it was taking so long to make a 'phone call. 'We have to get French insurance for the moped,' I called to him.

'Why, what have you done to it?' he asked.

I found a telephone box in a lock on Tuesday, by which time, it was Son's turn for the parental weekly bulletin. I couldn't reach Son; it was quite normal for the mobile telephone on his boat to be out of range when the tide was out at Woodbridge. Hoping that Berlin was free of tidal problems, I dialled Daughter's number.

'Where are you?' she asked, followed by, 'Can you make Strasbourg by Easter?' The suggestion was that she and our son-out-law drive from Berlin to spend Easter in Strasbourg with us.

'Can we make it?' I asked Peter. 'We've got twelve days.'

He thought we might make it if we travelled hard. 'We'll leave at crack of sparrows fart tomorrow,' he decreed.

Getting up early to go to Strasbourg for Easter seemed like a good idea before I went to bed. When I heard Peter get out of bed whilst it was still half dark, it seemed like a stupid idea.

Peter is one of those people that bounce around at the time of day when normal people pull duvets over their heads and groan. I'm of the latter ilk; the sound of tea bags crashing into tea pots gives me a headache. Peter clatters cups at an unacceptable noise pollution level and causes whistling kettles to shriek to migraine proportions. I could hear ours shrieking: *Give us a break here, it's only seven a.m.!*

When Peter leaned over my quilt shrouded head and noisily thumped a mug onto the bedside locker, I wondered why he was getting back into bed.

'Why are you getting back into bed?' I asked. 'What happened to crack of sparrows start?'

'I've got news for you,' said Peter, curling his icy cold legs round my warm ones. 'Sparrows don't fart when it's raining.'

Notwithstanding a small bird's reluctance towards flatulence in wet weather, we made good time. The weather was definitely improving, the flood water was on the wane and banks began to reassert themselves as river boundaries. A tiring but enjoyable nine hour travelling day brought us to Dun.

The receding water and diminishing current had probably induced the sculler onto the river. What induced him to fall asleep in the middle of the river, I can't imagine. We had just rounded a bend when we came across the stationary scull positioned sideways across our path. The slumped figure of a man suggested that the occupant of the craft might have died.

He nearly did – twice. Firstly because it took a lot of speedily applied reverse gear to avoid Colibri slicing the scull in half, and secondly because the blast of our hooter caused the man to throw his arms in the air in cardiac arrest precipitating fright. He must have been in shock to react the way he did. Grabbing his oars, he didn't – as was to be reasonably expected – move out of the way of a vast looming black shape. Instead, he propelled the scull in a complete circle, perilously close to Colibri's still advancing bow, before shooting down river ahead of us at a speed that could easily have dislodged the most experienced water skier.

'Phew! He's moving fast!' I said, as the tiny boat disappeared round a bend.

'Probably in a hurry to get back to the club house to change his trousers and hose out his boat,' was Peter's droll comment.

The guy in the rubber inner tube nearly had us reaching for clean pants. Always wary in stretches that announce themselves as water sports areas, Peter slowed Colibri to a gentle crawl on sighting a water ski notice.

We saw the speed boat heading towards us. The boat driver saw us in good time and swerved away. The occupant of the lorry tyre inner tube, which was attached to the speed boat by a hundred yards of rope, also saw us. His yell told us that, like us, he had also seen what was going to happen next. As the towing speed boat swung away in an arc, the inner tube hurtled towards us. There was nothing any of us could do, and I closed my eyes and waited for the inevitable. The sickening sound of a man's body crashing into our barge was preceded by screams from two girls in the speed boat. Unable to unlock my rigid limbs, with my eyes still closed, I asked Peter if he could see the man.

'No, he disappeared under our stern,' Peter's shaky voice informed me.

'The propeller – it'll chop him up!'

'No. I disengaged it in time – I think.'

The girls in the speed boat were still screaming. We looked fearfully over the side, expecting to see a pool of blood staining the water. I've heard people say a second can seem like an hour. We experienced a few of those sixty minute seconds before a man, still encased in a rubber inner tube, and still alive, emerged from beneath our stern, and floated to the surface. Although badly shaken, he was able to assure us that he was alright. Unbelievably, he even apologised!

We were relieved to reach Verdun and tie up. Sorry, Brian, a town mooring and a washing up bowl for you tonight. We'd had a traumatic day, and anyway, we didn't feel we could just simply pass through Verdun as well as Sedan. We were in an area of historical importance, even if that history was bloody. Cemeteries on the approach to Verdun are grim reminders of eight hundred thousand victims of what is rather strangely referred to as the Greatest battle of the 1914 – 1918 war. The town is interesting, and Peter, thinking that he would like to linger, asked me what time I had told the lock keeper we would depart next day. I told him nine o'clock.

'I'm tired,' Peter complained. 'We've been travelling in hard conditions for nearly two weeks; I could do with a lie in. Why do we always have to leave at nine o'clock in the morning?'

'Because,' I said, 'the lock keepers keep asking me what time we want to depart. And neuf heures is all I know in French.'

'If you only know that, how come you know what the lock keepers are asking?' Peter asked.

'It's the same thing I hear them say to you at the end of each day, and you always ask me what time we'll be leaving in the morning,' I said. 'Don't worry, I'll learn French.'

'In that case, he's not a lock keeper, he's an eclusier,' Peter informed me.

'Sure, and a pompier is a bloody fireman.'

'How do you know that?'

'I just do, there's a song about it. Come on, it's nearly neuf heures.'

'Okay, calm down.'

'Don't tell me to calm down. I'm tired, we've been travelling in hard conditions for nearly two weeks.' As I stomped off, I could hear Peter singing: Où est la pompier?

Later that day, after Peter had arranged with the lock keeper – sorry, eclusier – to leave at ten in the morning, he sat me down, put a glass in my hand and taught me: deize heures, onze heures – onze heures a demi even.

I still insist it wasn't entirely my fault that I got my deize and my douze mixed up. It was my first French lesson – and it could have been worse. We could have arrived at a lock two hours late instead of having to wait two hours for twelve o'clock.

It certainly wasn't my fault the gear box failed in the next lock. In fact, when I heard Peter yell, 'We've lost gears!' my immediate reaction was one of indifference. We were nearly in the lock, we didn't need to drive anywhere for a few minutes, and, anyway, I wasn't speaking to him until he apologised.

Then I clicked into the panic note in Peter's voice. No gears meant no reverse. No reverse meant no stopping – and we were speedily approaching the far lock gates! With a presence of mind that stunned even me, I lunged at a bollard and dropped a loop onto it before leaping backwards out of the way. The rope strained against the weight of a hundred tons, twitched and shuddered, but held long enough to bring Colibri to a halt before she shot out the other end of the lock wearing a pair of gates draped across her bow.

Such was Peter's admiration for my fast action, that he granted me full impunity for my time muddling of earlier. I bought some beautiful big brown eggs from the lock keeper's wife, to make amends for threatening her husband's gates, and to make an omelette for supper. She was unaware that we had come close to scrambling the gates, but I bet she knew what wonderful scrambled eggs she afforded us.

Enjoying welcome spring warmth, we continued upstream to the summit, where we would have to pass through the Foug Tunnel before travelling down hill to the Moselle. Leaving bright sunshine behind, we entered the half mile long tunnel, relieved to find it was lit. Wind and rain greeted us on our exit, and we found ourselves confronted by two locks. How were we supposed to know which one to enter? A strong gust of wind moved us to the right. We went for the right hand lock.

A man scurried from the control shed and lifted my rope loop off the lock bollard. Uh-oh, this looked like we had chosen the wrong lock. No, the man kindly passed my rope round the bollard and handed the loop to me, patiently explaining that, when we were way down in his very deep lock, I wouldn't be able to retrieve my loop from way above my head. Good point, and obvious of course – even to the dimmest bargee. But this dim bargee had been travelling up in locks since Namur, and her brain had gone into storage with the excuse of being tired, cold and wet. Hoping that my bright smile was visible through the murky rain, I thanked the man. He wagged an admonishing finger at me, which seemed to imply that he would forgive me my stupidity this time, but I shouldn't make a habit of it.

With a strong wind and a peculiar undertow from the lock sluices fighting against us, we crashed our way through three down hill locks. Once in the chain of these close together locks, it is normally expected that a boat will complete the chain. However, Peter decided that he was too tired and conditions too poor for him to continue safely. The lock keeper who had been assigned to escort us, readily agreed with that decision and went home early.

Sunshine accompanied us through the remainder of the Toul locks next morning, and we turned, with great pleasure, onto the Moselle. Although a canalised section rather than the Moselle river as such, it was wide and deep and a pleasure to navigate.

The turn into the Marne au Rhin Canal was less easy. I'm not too sure how we got into it at all. Sun in our eyes didn't assist in spotting the turning and, once spotted, it wasn't obvious exactly where we should go. A long bridge, like a tunnel, obscured sight of the lock itself. We plunged from bright sunlight into darkness, not really sure what was in front of us. It was probably a case of the lock finding us.

The start of this new canal was uninspiring. We didn't fancy Nancy. A beautiful town, we are told, but it hides this fact from canal users, who are offered a dingy aspect as the canal skirts the town through the tradesman's entrance. It offers ample scope for boat mooring, but the weather seemed to dull in sympathy with the scenery, and rain didn't invite a walk to the pretty part. Beyond Nancy, the canal runs through unpretty industrial areas – which are, of course, the reason for the canal's existence, but do not make for pleasant cruising.

The ambience improved as we cruised on, but we missed the friendliness of lock keepers. At one stage, I was given a little plastic box that looked like the devices that hospital housemen wear poking out of white jacket pockets. The things that beep when the a doctor is required to be somewhere other than where he is. These ones were designed to inform a lock that you wanted to use it. I stood on the bow, happily zapping electronic gear on poles that incongruously protruded from rural river banks, until one I fired at failed to respond. I yelled at Peter that he would have to go back so I could zap again. He had what he called a better idea, he would put me off at the bank so I could walk back to the pole. I topped that with an even better idea. I asked an approaching boat crew to zap on their way past.

Onward ever onward with Easter and Strasbourg getting closer. We knew all about the Ronquieres inclined plane; we were prepared for the Arzviller inclined plane that waited beyond two tunnel sections. We were not, however, prepared for the spectacular rocky scenery that reared up at us as we left the tunnels, or the view of the Zorn Valley that lay below and presented itself as we approached the plane.

We conveniently presented ourselves as a another tourist attraction. A coach load of guided tourists clustered around the entrance to the tank, and their guide gave a commentary on Colibri, adding the riveting fact that the plane and canals had been constructed for barges of this type. The tourists probably thought we had been arranged for their benefit, and we entered the tank amid cheers and camera clicking. I called out, 'Split the tips with us,' to a guide who appeared not to understand English.

All this distracted us from noticing that, although we entered a similar tank to the ones at Ronquieres, this one differed in that, beyond normal looking lock gates at the far end, was a tree dotted hillside. No water, no clue as to what we would do when those gates opened – just a tree dotted hillside. Neither of us wanted to be the one to appear stupid by mentioning this phenomenon. Both of us were glad we hadn't when the tank began to carry us – sideways – down into the valley, where a perfectly normal looking ribbon of water awaited to carry us to Strasbourg.

Sparrows paled into insignificance here, where storks are considered normal local fauna. When I saw the size of their nests, I was relieved that we looked like reaching our goal without their early morning assistance. And we did. We made it, in spite of snow. Two days before Good Friday, we were a day away from Strasbourg. I 'phoned Daughter from the delightful little town of Saverne.

We did understand, really we did. Whilst the Zorn Valley looked very pretty under a mantle of white, snow bound autobahns between Berlin and Strasbourg held less appeal.

Chapter Eleven

SLOW DOWN – I WANT TO ENJOY THIS

When we left Brussels – was it really only three weeks ago! – we had no idea that we would be in the Alsace in the middle of April. We hadn't started out with any particular plan beyond going to France. France is a big country, with hundreds of miles of inland waterways, but we had given little thought to where to explore or in what order. The Alsace just sort of entered the itinerary, courtesy of one defaulting daughter. But that was the wonder and beauty of this whole adventure; it didn't matter where we went, or when. Saverne was a very nice place to pause for thought and plan our next move. Meanwhile, it was pleasant to rest, and to gaze in awe across the harbour at a chateau bathed in rose tinted flood lights.

We chatted to a chateau gazing English family on a hire boat. They were nearing the end of their week's cruise, and would be leaving to spend a week in a gite in Burgundy. 'Burgundy is beautiful,' I said. 'We're going there too.'

This gave Peter his turn to say: 'Are we?'

'Why not? Burgundy is beautiful, and we do have to take Colibri to her scene of conception. Anyway, it's probably warmer there,' I reasoned.

The obvious route from Strasbourg to Burgundy is via the the Rhine and the Grand Canal de Alsace. Our book gave dimensions of locks designed to accommodate huge commercial ships – several, in one go. It also gave hints about strong current and navigation difficulties. We didn't need any of that. We felt we had already tackled enough rough conditions to satisfy any requirement for excitement and adrenaline kicks. Having passed through the Marne au Rhin canal so quickly to get here, we were inclined to return at a more leisurely pace.

Peter turned Colibri round – nothing to it these days – and I piled wood on the fire to make sure it would keep going whist we travelled. So much smoke belched from our chimney as we entered the deep Saverne lock that it completely obscured Peter's vision. Smoke filled the lock, crawled up the walls and escaped in a billowing cloud at street level. Coughing spectators backed off from a lock that had adopted the characteristics of a smouldering volcano. Serve them right; not one of them offered to take my rope. I was forced to climb up an eighteen foot ladder through the smoke with a rope over my shoulder, feeling like a volunteer reserve fireman practising for the real thing.

Snow or not, this was Easter week, and the hire boats were out. Only slightly daunted by coping with Arctic conditions in a fibre glass boat, people were exploring the superb Alsace countryside. We had, of course, met hire boats on the Canal du Midi, when Tiger Lily had jostled with them for lock space. Those were crewed by tanned, shorts or bikini clad bodies, in South of France August temperatures. It hadn't occurred to us that people did it in the Alsace in snow!

These were a different breed of boaters; intrepid, hardy all weather types, bravely driving unfamiliar boats in and out of locks – unless a big barge obstructed their passage. Compared to Belgium and Holland, far fewer commercial barges were in evidence. When one does appear, it is normal practice to give way, and allow it to precede a pleasure boat into a lock. In our case, although a barge, we took our rightful turn with the holiday makers. It really wasn't our fault that we brought traffic to a standstill for nearly an hour.

The Zorn Valley locks are smartly painted and sophisticated. No friendly keepers to open and close one gate while you do the other; the gates open and close automatically. Well . . . they do usually. This was our twenty somethingth lock of this type, and we entered with smug *been here, done that* complacency. I nonchalantly tweaked the blue lever. I then gave the blue lever a hard yank, followed by a rising panic induced even harder yank. Sophisticated automatic lock operating machinery remained stubornly unwilling to operate. The gates had closed behind us, and we were captive inside a lock that had no intention of allowing us to escape.

An irate hire boater came to see why we were hogging a lock he was rather anxious to use. He pompously informed me that it was necessary to operate the blue lever. I offered him the opportunity to show me how. 'It is kaput,' he announced. 'What have you done?'

Boats formed a queue both ends of the lock. Boaters came to see what the delay was. They clucked sympathetic noises at our plight of being trapped by an over functioning temper in a malfunctioning lock.

'I have waited twenty minutes for this ship,' the irate man informed a Swiss lady. He was obviously in a hurry to complete his cruise and return to Germany. Meanwhile, European relations were hardly enhanced by the fact that Dillon, from her cage in our wheelhouse, chose that moment to say: 'So what?'

'I have been on this canal three days,' the irate one informed a Dutchman. 'I have come from Strasbourg since Sunday, and this is not occurring before!'

The man's temper was not cooled by Dillon's next comment: 'I am a sod!' or by the subsequent laughter, which Dillon joined in. Unfortunately, it is my raucous laugh that she uses on these occasions, so I just smiled weakly and pretended that this had nothing to do with me.

The Swiss lady asked me how long we had been on our boat. 'Two and a half years,' I replied. 'We have come from Northern Holland and, actually, this has not occurred to us before either.'

'Ships like this are too big for these canals!' was the slightly deflated Germanic parting shot as leather boots heavily stomped away.

'Go slap your leder hosen,' called the Dutchman – which rather overshadowed my mild comment that these canals were actually built for ships like ours.

We were liberated by a trouble shooting eclusier who arrived in a van. The illusion that boats were left to fend for themselves was dispersed as the cheerful Frenchman fiddled with knobs in a control box, causing the lock to function smoothly, and in favour of the more amiable boaters, who would pass through whilst the other sort waited for the lock to open at his end. Despite the latter's attitude, as British crew on a Belgian registered Dutch barge travelling in France, we hoped that the one big happy family of a combined Europe would happen one day.

We stopped at Lutzelbourg; I believe most people do. With it's splendid church that graces so many postcards, it is among the prettiest canal side villages to be found in France. Someone we met there told us we should have stopped in Nancy, apparently one of the most beautiful cities France boasts. We would be passing through again; maybe we would linger this time. Meanwhile, retracing our steps through the densely pine clad hillsides of the Zorn valley, we rode up in the inclined plane to more camera snapping and video recorder whirring. I began to wish we had a dollar for every roll of film on which Colibri entered America.

The tunnel's lights were green, and we entered without delay. It was the sound of music that alerted us to the fact that we were not alone. Looking behind, we could see no boats following. Nothing could be coming towards us; the tunnel carried one way traffic only.

Wrong – the tunnel is *supposed* to carry one way traffic only, but something was definitely coming towards us. Nearing the end, we were able to see a boat in the daylight that poured through the tunnel exit.

The driver of the advancing boat was presumably unable to see us in the dark, but evidence that he heard our hooter – grossly amplified by the tunnel's acoustics – was immediate. An attempted quick turn around proved that the tunnel was not as wide as the little boat was long. Finding his boat wedged across the tunnel, the driver went for furious throttle application, resulting in his bow being even more firmly embedded in the tunnel wall. The pressure of an abundance of arms and legs attained the boats release from it's stone straight jacket, and the multi limb application held it from the wall as it reversed into the sunlight. The boat popped out of the tunnel entrance, and we could hear agitated voices above the music emanating from a deck top speaker as flailing arms became impotent. Now the driver achieved his quick turn around – three times in all – before a crew member launched himself towards land during a bank bouncing part of the sequence. He had reached the water's edge and was squelching his way up the bank when another crew member threw him what looked like a bundle of knitting wool. The next bank bounce ejected a third crew member, who hastily assisted in the untangling of knitting wool task. With the two bank side men acting as shore bollards, and a girl on the boat hanging onto her end of rope with grim determination, we eased round the stern of their boat and out of their way. I couldn't resist pointing to the red no entry light as we passed.

Wintery weather persisted, so we took time out to strip the aft quarters. It seemed preferable to me hanging out of the wheelhouse to scrape sleet from the windscreen so Peter could see where he was going.

With the intention of rebuilding the aft quarters into a snug, well insulated little self contained nest, we first had to dispose of sixty years worth of peeling varnished woodwork; some of which was left in huge wheelie bins en route. I kept trying to throw out scraps of scruffy wood, only to have Peter grab it from me, declaring that it was sixty year old teak. 'You can't buy wood like that!' he informed me.

'Can you buy wood like this?' I asked, holding up a piece of rust stained grey timber.

'You can light the fire with that, it's only softwood,' I was told.

Huh, all wood feels hard to me; I'm blowed if I could tell the difference between old teak and modern two by one when it all carries the same heavy disguise of layers of orange varnish.

Considering that we were supposed to be clearing the area, we ended up walking round a heap of wonderfully mature solid teak, which left us with less space than we started with. It was unfortunate that, standing on a sixty year old nail sticking out of a sixty year old bit of hardwood, a forty eight year old woman's shriek caused her husband to topple from a little blue stool whilst clutching a ceiling panel he had been carefully prising off. Peter's shrieks joined my intensified ones as we collapsed beneath splintered wood and a cloud of sixty year old dust.

Extricating ourselves from a scattered heap of sharp instrument encrusted precious teak, we agreed that we couldn't continue to work in the ever decreasing space. The plan to de-nail, de-hinge, de-screw and de-doorknob the pieces so we could stack them neatly was cancelled by the sudden arrival of the hitherto hesitant spring. The construction of this barge had dominated our lives for more than two years. We had taken time out to cruise; the weather was glorious so we went back to cruising.

Still didn't fancy Nancy. We passed through her back door again; it wasn't city weather. Maybe we would return one day in the right meteorological conditions. Maybe we would return by car and enter by the front door. Meanwhile, it was weather for gently gliding along the sparkling sunlit Moselle.

Sparkle is what it did. After the narrow confines of the concrete canal we had just left, we revelled in the openness of wide clear water and far reaching vistas of gentle countryside. Trees and bushes, wearing the soft greens of new spring growth, rose from lush banks splashed with coloured patches of wild flowers and blended with the dark greens of distant conifers.

It was a day for standing on the deck of a gently gliding boat, with a soft warm breeze caressing a face lifted to an unending expanse of clear blue sky. I stretched out my arms and, between deep draughts of fresh, clean air, I called, 'Come and look at the world!'

Leaving the wheel to fend for itself, Peter joined me on deck. When Colibri looked as if she was planning to moor herself at a piece of bank she fancied, Peter told me to stop being a hedonist and go and be a barge driver. He settled himself in one of Adrian's garden chairs and announced that he was never going back to work at a noisy polluted airport.

Relaxed, sunburned and happy after our day on the Moselle, we resisted the urge to stop at Sexey Aux Forges and arrived at the Canal de l'Est as the sun was sinking.

The Canal de l'est Branch Sud is delightful. Unlike it's big brother, the Branch Nord, it is a true French canal. Passing through the first lock, we felt we had found the cruising ground that we had hankered after since travelling through France on Tiger Lily. Colibri was guided in and out of Freycinet gauge locks, a mere few inches wider than her beam. A different, but invariably cheerful, lock keeper escorted us each day. I became adept at leaping off the boat to close one gate whilst our lock keeper closed the other. Once we had jointly opened the far gates, the lock keeper rode ahead on a bike or a moped to await us at the next lock.

This canal closed on Sundays, so Saturday afternoon, we looked out for a nice place to spend a day of rest. We chose a shady bank at a point where the river nudges the canal. Banging metal stakes into the ground to hold ropes, we settled beneath trees. Carrying glasses and a bottle, we walked a few steps across the towpath to sit beside the real River Moselle. Narrow and gently flowing, the pretty river meanders through twists and turns, keeping company with the canal for much of the way between Neuves Maison and Epinal. Glimpses of it add enchantment to this route. None of which interested Brian in the least – he was just blissfully happy to have a whole day to roam freely on a deserted sunny bank. He rolled in warm grass, shinned up a few trees, chased a few lizards then sunned himself on the wheelhouse roof.

Early evening lightning flashes altered our barbecue plans. Instead, we took grandstand seats in the wheelhouse and, with plates of egg and chips washed down with Alsace wine, watched a dramatic storm lash itself into a frenzy against the backdrop of Vosges mountains. Torrential rain and spectacular lightning gave an impressive performance to accompanying cannon booming thunder. The only thing missing was the 1812 Overture soundtrack.

Our lock keeper was faithfully in position, in drenching rain, for our neuf heures appointment Monday morning. This was a disadvantage of a highly efficiently run canal; making arrangements in advance didn't leave scope for changes of plan. We would have preferred not to travel in pouring rain, but had no way to cancel our appointment with a lock keeper who would have preferred not to keep locks in pouring rain.

Our man of today gallantly, cheerfully even, carried out his duties, but we felt guilty about him working in such awful weather conditions. As we neared the fourth lock of the morning, I watched in dismay as the lock keeper opened one gate, ran the length of the lock, sprinted across the far gates and ran the length of the lock on the other side to open the second gate in time for our arrival. He then slumped over the gate handle, with rain pouring off his anorak hood and down his face.

'Enough,' we said. None of us wanted to be doing this today. Taking a dripping man into the wheelhouse, putting a mug of hot coffee into his stiff fingers, we told him we wanted to stop, and suggested that he go home and change into dry clothes. He was obviously relieved, but also concerned. We had booked him for the day; he was supposed to stay with us, whatever the weather. He insisted on taking us through one more lock to where there was a good place for us to rest. 'Very good,' he promised. 'Free water and electricity for barges.'

We didn't care where we stopped. Right here, in this lock

would have satisfied me, but we agreed to be led to the promised land. Pleased with our cooperation, he stepped out of the puddle he had created on the wheelhouse floor and roared off on his moped; doing a Barry Sheen act down a towpath that looked more like a muddy stream. Once through the next lock, with a soggy *follow me* gesture and his moped slowed to match our pace, our valiant out rider led us to Charme. With rain bucketing down on his head, he stood beside the bollard he had chosen for us. With this super guy's assistance, we were safely and snugly moored within minutes. Only then did he leave us, satisfied that he had done the best he could for these English whimps that were daunted by a bit of torrential rain.

We had heard about the Golby Flight. Fourteen locks in two miles promised heavy work for a two person crewed barge. Our chart told us that three to five hours should be allowed, and that we should report in and take our place in the queue.

What queue? Colibri was the only boat offering itself for the endurance test that morning. Obviously an ordeal which is taken seriously because we were allocated two lock keepers to assist us through.

The one in the knee high leather boots, peaked cap and pseudo military jacket seemed to have a power complex. Or maybe he was only practising for the militia. His amiable side kick wore wellies and denim and rode a pedal cycle with a chain that rattled against what was left of a rusty chain guard. The commandant had a much superior steed. His black moped, polished and buffed to parade ground standards, stood meekly to attention while its master briefed us. We must move quickly. A commercial barge was close behind, and would be much displeased to be delayed by a craft indulging in mere pleasure. Peter asked the number two how far behind the impatient commercial was. With a shrug, he admitted that it was twenty minutes away.

The peremptory beckoning of the commanding officer as we moved from lock to lock, and his tongue clicking demands to move quickly, were beginning to ruffle my calm by the fifth lock. I kept looking behind, expecting to see a fire breathing commercial barge irately bearing down on us.

'How far behind is the other barge now?' Peter asked the amiable one.

Another shrug and: 'Perhaps, forty minutes.'

'So what's the hurry?'

The predictable shrug and an expressive tilt of head towards the Operation Commander.

'If your chief wants this boat to move faster, he can drive it while I do his job,' Peter retorted.

This elicited, not a negative shrug, but a positive chortle. The bike chain clanked and another bit of rusted chain guard bit the dust as a subordinate lock keeper pedalled off at speed to impart this gem to his superior officer. At least, we assume that happened because of the latter's sudden change of attitude. Monsieur Officious suddenly became Monsieur Ultra-Jocular, and told us how well we were coping with his difficult locks.

'Pouf!' he exclaimed. 'The other barge will be far behind by the time *we* reach the end.'

This new spirit of camaraderie had the effect of us all wanting to prove Colibri's performance. Imperious beckoning became encouraging urging. Tongue was now clicked in approval, and we were kept informed of just how far behind the labouring commercial was lagging. When we entered the fourteenth and final lock, two hours and fifty minutes after entering the first one, we were the recipients of celebratory hand shaking and shoulder slapping.

'A peniche takes at least four hours!' a delighted Commander in Chief told us.

'Sometimes as many as six,' added his panting assistant – with a shrug.

After some shared beers, we waved goodbye with the feeling that our new found partner in our new found excellence was expecting to gain kudos when he boasted about how he got a peniche through the Golby Flight in less than three hours.

Our delight in this canal increased as we twisted and turned through to the heavily wooded summit. Beyond the summit, we entered the sort of world that dreams are made of. Each time we went down in a lock, the far gates slowly opened to reveal yet another vista of breathtaking beauty. Birds twittered and called constantly in dense woods. Herons stood and watched our approach. When our bow was level with them, they took off, flew ahead and waited on the bank for us to catch up before flying ahead again. This was obviously a standard heron game; it enchanted us.

I was also enchanted by the abundance of wild spring flowers. Some I recognized, others I had never seen before. Enacting my dotty English lady dream, I wandered towpaths and picked flowers. I now had time in my life for vases of flowers as well as jars of paint brushes in white spirit. What I didn't have was any vases. A tiny, slim necked cream bottle served to hold a single stem of a multi headed, brightly coloured flower. A marmalade jar substituted for the crystal glass vase that a selection of delicate blooms deserved.

Peter watched my enjoyment, felt that I had recently missed out on a few of the niceties that a woman gains pleasure from, and was concerned that I had no beautiful vases in my life. No, he didn't rush out and buy me crystal glass and porcelain; he found a can of matt black spray paint in the engine room and sprayed my marmalade jar for me. It looked lovely, and I immediately applied the spray treatment to the cream bottle.

Over the next few days, I sprayed an assortment of jam and peanut butter jars and sauce bottles. I hesitated over a Paul Masson wine carafe from the days when we bought Californian wine. I had kept it, thinking it would make a good emergency urine bottle if Peter ever became bed bound. What the hell, a matt black urine bottle was every bit as serviceable as a clear glass one – and Peter wasn't showing signs of becoming bed bound anyway. Meanwhile, sprayed matt black, the carafe made an elegant receptacle for those bushy purple tinged grasses that grew on the banks. Bored with vases, I turned my attention and spray nozzle towards anything that had plant pot potential.

Peter eventually confiscated my can of spray paint before everything on board became a matt black shadow of it's former self.

The little town of Fontenoy le Chateau was as nice as it sounds. Other boaters thought so too, and Colibri was squeezed into a mooring that, just a few weeks ago, would have been dismissed as too difficult. I thought it was too difficult to get out of this tight space when a Dutch commercial barge moored alongside us. In fact, I just sort of assumed we would stay in Fontenoy le Chateau until the commercial moved on. However, the Dutch people were planning to stay a few days.

'We're moving out,' said Peter, after conferring with the barge skipper.

'How?' I wanted to know.

'The other barge will push it's stern out into the middle of the canal, and we'll pull out backwards,' was explained to me.

'What! Out and round the restaurant barge behind, through a gap between it and the commercial – backwards!'

'That's right. Take our ropes off will you?'

'What – now?'

'Now.'

The interested audience this manoeuvre attracted did nothing to soothe my agitation. Several photographs were taken of me chewing the end of my new white nylon rope as I stood on the foredeck, facing away from the action, trying to pretend that this wasn't happening. Frau Bargee, with admirable cool, roped the front of her barge into the space we vacated, playing her two inch thick ropes like silken threads.

The scraping and crunching of metal I awaited didn't happen. The stern of the other barge slid, within inches of our bow, and gently landed alongside the bank. Daring to cast a surreptitious glance behind, I was amazed to see we were floating free and nosing into the middle of the canal.

I became calmer after Peter had drunk a strong cup of coffee. 'That was enough nerve wracking excitement to last a while,' I said, as we rounded a sharp bend and were almost immediately confronted by a narrow bridge – the aperture of which we were not exactly on course for.

While Peter did some frenzied juggling with forward and reverse gear, trying to straighten Colibri in a confined space, my attention was caught by the grinning face of a small boy hanging over the bridge parapet. The kid positively gloated, not taking his eyes off Colibri's bow approaching the bridge. He knew exactly what was coming. We didn't disappoint him. We hit the bridge. Our bow glanced the stonework, bounced off and grazed the other side; adding some of our paint work to the multi hued streaks that were testimony to the passing of many barges over many years.

We knew the little boy was pleased because he cheered, clapped and gave us the thumbs up sign. Other small kids spend their time train spotting. This little brat's hobby was barges hitting bridges spotting. And he kept notes. I know he did because I saw a bulging note book stuffed down the V of his jumper. He probably recorded barge name, date, time of impact and decibels registered. I wonder if, to our notes, he added: There was a strange lady on deck who curtsied and stuck out her tongue.

We emerged the other side of the bridge, and I turned to wave goodbye to the little lad, thinking: One day, a sodding great barge will thump that bridge so hard, that one small boy and his note book will be catapulted into the canal.

Congratulating ourselves on passing that obstacle without the need for major dent removing surgery, we trundled on; only to find another bridge obstructively placed before us. We were not going to get through that one – it was one of those knee high, street level jobs, with cars shooting across a couple of feet above the canal.

Consulting the chart, we learned that a radar detector would alert the bridge to our need to pass, whereupon, it would stop the traffic and rise in the air. This didn't happen for us. After ten minutes, we decided to moor up whilst we waited. I spied a metal grid in the canal wall, which I thought I would be able to catch hold of it with a hook on the end of a rope. This was accomplished quite smoothly, and we settled down to wait for the bridge to acknowledge our presence.

It was a well informed passer by who passed on the knowledge that we like to think he gained from other stupid boaters. He told us we must pass the metal grid, not moor to it. Why? Because the radar detector was lurking behind that grid – and was holding it's breath waiting for us to pass so it could relay a moving shape message to the bridge.

With a feeling of regret that we would soon be leaving this enchanted canal, we neared the former Gallo Roman settlement at Corre. There we turned off the Canal de l'est and skidded onto the River Saone. Feeling a river flow beneath the hull after seventy five miles of current free canal was weird.

'I wish this thing had brakes,' said Peter, as we seemed to hurtle at ten miles an hour towards a porte de garde. Safely through, we spotted two bollards by a waterside village that looked mellow and attractive in the afternoon sun. It also looked as if it would have a bakery, so we stopped for a loaf of bread and a spot of exploration.

Walking through the village of Ormoy, we were fascinated by a mixture of well kept houses juxtapositional with apparently derelict buildings. I pointed at a particularly picturesque cottage. Gaily flowered window boxes, flanked by red painted shutters set against sparkling white stone walls presented a charming picture. We nodded in appreciation, then Peter pointed to the peeling shutters and drooping guttering of the ramshackle assembly of grey stonework that hung onto the side of the pretty cottage. We shook heads in puzzlement before moving on to point at the village square, where we stood and stared at the quaint church.

Later, eating supper in the wheelhouse, I had a feeling that we were being watched. Two women and a child stood on the bank, staring at Colibri. They were joined by a man and a dog, then three other people, all of whom pointed and stared at our home. It was only fair. We had walked round their village pointing and staring. It was the natives' turn to come to have a look at us. At least they were very friendly.

There had been no need for us to feel sad at leaving the canal. The upper reaches of the River Saone came close to being equally enchanting. A narrow stretch ran between heavily wooded banks before widening into a larger river. Current and weirs re-entered our lives and, tucked away to one side, locks appeared suddenly, taking us by surprise. Countryside became more open and undulating as we floated through towns and villages, past an impressive castle at Ray-Sur-Saone, and on towards Burgundy.

Before we achieved the entry into Burgundy, we blotted our copy book at Gray. Such was the gravity of our misdemeanour, that the lock keeper at Gray took our name!

There is no protective lock cut above this lock. Entry to it is from beside a sizeable weir that commands respect. Unluckily, we met a commercial barge that failed to respect our situation, and commanded that we reverse from it's path. There was actually ample room for the barge to pass us, but it didn't want to pass, it wanted to moor where we waited. Peter was forced to reverse Colibri above the weir, which was crashing tumultuously to the river level six feet or so below. But for experience gained on flooded Belgian rivers, we may well have come in for a spot of white water rafting.

Meanwhile, the lock keeper was jumping up and down. Our eventual entry to his lock was made to his vociferous quoting of his personal creed, on the lines of: Thou shalt bow down and afford holy grace to commercial shipping, regardless of their behaviour and your own safety. This was when we suffered the football field humiliation of having our names taken – well, Peter's and Colibri's anyway, mine was apparently of no consequence. Monsieur Eclusier de Ecluse de Gray produced a note book that our little lad on the bridge would have been proud of. With a dramatic flourish of a stubby pencil, Colibri was added to hundreds of entries in the misconduct file, together with date and time of committed offence. Undoubtedly, our details jostled for space with many a worthy boat that, over many years, had violated this eclusier's code. In fact, entry in the Gray lock keeper's sin book probably qualified us for membership of some esoteric society that no self respecting boater would admit to being excluded from.

After that fracas, the bliss of our overnight mooring was balm to troubled souls. Tucked into a bend of the now much wider river, was a pontoon. A square of carpet and a notice on this unexpected landing stage spelled a welcome for passing boats. What a glorious place to be welcomed to. Beside the pontoon, on the edge of woods, stood a stone picnic table and benches. The woods invited strolling through, and Brian voted for this little bit of paradise by leaping ashore before mooring was completed. Whilst we ate our evening meal at the stone table, the parrots tried to out do the bird calls that were the only disturbance to utter tranquillity.

We had arrived in Burgundy. We felt comfortable and happy to be here.

Awaking to brilliant sunshine peeping through trees and making leaf patterns on deck, we felt unable to move from this idyllic place. A morning walking through the woods with one very happy cat preceded pancakes for lunch; cooked and tossed over the barbecue. A siesta, followed by firewood gleaning, led to an al fresco evening meal. We were settling down at the stone table to enjoy a charcoaled feast when a gleaming Renault Espace suddenly appeared through the trees. The jacketed and bow tied driver was looking for a boat party that had booked a restaurant table. So, if Peter hadn't felt like slaving over a hot barbecue, all we had to do was call this restaurant in nearby Pesmes, and a car would have been sent to fetch us. Wonderful. We took the driver's card for future reference, and wished him luck in finding the boat that hungrily awaited his services.

If we had been able to find the supposedly nearby village, we may well have stayed indefinitely. But, after breakfast pancakes made over rekindled charcoal, the little barbecue was loaded on deck. Breadless, we drifted down river to St. Jean de Losne. Our faces and bare legs were already acquiring a brown sheen, and summer stretched ahead of us.

I made a mental note to buy dried yeast in St. Jean de Losne. Man cannot live on pancakes alone.

Chapter Twelve

FLACID DRAPEAU

Turning off the River Saone, we entered the Canal du Bourgogne. The same lock keeper admitted us as, for the first time, we repeated a lock that we had passed through on Tiger Lily.

St. Jean de Losne was just as we remembered it. We found it rather nice to be among other boats, and to talk with someone other than each other and two parrots. It was so hot in the port that the parrots held their wings away from their bodies and came as close as parrots can to panting. We took the wheelhouse roof off and sprayed the drooping birds with cool water before making several cycle trips to two supermarkets. With memories of a dearth of shops on this route, we piled basic supplies on board and relished the prospect of retracing Tiger Lily's steps to the point where she suffered the metamorphous of becoming a Dutch barge in our minds.

Would the log tables and the matchstick men still be there? We would find out in seventy four locks time. But there was no hurry; we had weeks in which to travel a distance that could be covered in a little over an hour by car.

The neuf heures starts dissolved into timeless, appointment free travel. No one cared what time we arrived at our first lock of the day – or even if we arrived at all. Leisurely breakfasts were followed by a few locks before a leisurely lunch in the shade of trees. Some lunch breaks extended to the next day as somnambulant afternoons stretched into warm, balmy evenings. Time had no meaning, and the date even less. I discovered what day of the week it was when I cycled off in search of bread. A notice on the shuttered door of the boulangerie I found said: Ferme a Lundi.

'Where's the bread?' asked Peter when I returned with sunflowers across my handlebars, 'I'm not keen on pate on petals.'

'Shop's closed on Mondays,' I cheerily informed him.

'How do you know it's Monday?'

'Is Lundi Monday?'

'Yes.'

'Then it's Monday today.'

'Is it really? Which Monday?'

'How should I know? I think it's still June though.'

Tourists were out and about, enjoying the delights of Burgundy in Summer. We became used to being questioned by strangers who wanted to know where we had come from, where we were going and why. When we had been interviewed half a dozen times, I considered making a tape recording of the standard answers to the standard questions. But I decided against that scheme; we were enjoying talking to people who were interested in our barge and in what we were doing. We met them in locks, or as they strolled or cycled past our bankside mooring. Cars stopped to take photographs of Colibri moving along the canal, then drove to the next lock for shots of her in a lock and for conversation with us.

We worked out a one to ten scale of interest between a few casual questions and a full scale inquisition and came up with the ten minute criterion. If people were still talking to us after ten minutes, they were invited on board to view the barge. Or if they were still firing questions from the lockside when it was time for us to move out, they were invited to travel on board to the next lock.

We met some nice people, and we later received Christmas cards from some; including one that said: Hi, remember us? We're the couple in the red Metro who came on board for a few minutes and stayed all day. Yes, we did remember them, and the few hours in their very pleasant company over a few glasses of wine. Other people kindly sent photographs they had taken of Colibri, us, us beside Colibri etc. One couple, with whom we spent an enjoyable couple of hours on deck, sent a book about barging in Burgundy. People are allowed to read that book on board, but no one is permitted a take away borrow.

A few times, German tourists spoke to us in German. I was bemused when a man I had heard speaking to his child in French, asked a question that left me guessing as to the content. He repeated the question, obviously struggling to deliver words that I vaguely recognized as being possibly from the German language. Sure that my French would be just as vaguely recognizable, I chose English to tell this man that I didn't speak German. When he said, 'But, your drapeau is showing,' I noted his hint of surprise. I was feeling some of that as well, not to mention a tinge of concern. I wasn't wearing a petticoat, my knickers were firmly harnessed within my shorts, and a surreptitious fingering of upper lip confirmed that my nose was not misbehaving. What the devil was my drapeau – and was it an offence to be showing it?

The man pointed to the flag hanging limply from it's pole. 'Your drapeau it show German, no?'

As I explained that, no, my flag was Belgian, I could see that, when clinging to the flag pole, the vertical black, yellow and red Belgian stripes looked like the horizontal black, red and yellow stripes of the German flag.

Peter did look a bit startled when I suggested that we either hold his flaccid drapeau erect with stiff wire or remove it completely. His answer was to opt for the Belgian protocol of flying the flag of the proprietor. We would have been reluctant to do so at sea, but here, in a snug little inland waterway, we raised the British Red Ensign and drank a toast in French wine.

We ambled happily through the Bourgogne Canal, slowing down to virtual standstill in the Ouche Valley. Above Dijon, a motorway thundering alongside the canal reminded us of M25 days and a former life. We waved back to drivers that hooted greeting as they flashed past. A coach, displaying British registration plates and a banner announcing a Spanish destination, slowed down, hooting raucously. The inmates waved and offered the thumbs up sign. Humbly thankful for our life in the slow lane, we cruised on to find a peaceful night time mooring. We found it at Fleurey sur Ouche.

The charm of the picturesque village of Fleurey held us captive for a few days. I shook dust from a long untouched box of books and stretched out under trees beside the little River Ouche. Peter rummaged in the forepeak, searching through stuff that he had never had time to investigate, and emerged dusty and bearing a wooden box of what he called treasures. I looked briefly into the box and announced it to contain unidentifiable junk. Lumps of glass and assorted oddments didn't hold my attention but, like a kid playing with Meccano, Peter assembled a set of pre war navigation lights. I left him to it and went below to wash up, only to be summoned to: Come and look at this.

"This" was an old oil lamp, reconstructed from various components the treasure box had yielded. Even I could see that, with the brass bits and the tall bulbous glass cleaned, it would be a nice object. Leaving Peter trimming his wick, I went back to domestics.

'I need some oil,' said Peter, moving me aside to get to the under sink cupboard.

'In the chip pan,' I told him.

'No, not that sort of oil. I'm going to be a wise virgin and fill my lamp with oil.'

'If you'd like to have a go at some good husbandry and dry up for me, I'll help you look.'

That evening, after the sun disappeared, we sat on deck in the warm glow of an authentically ancient oil lamp. When the evening air became chilly, we moved into the wheelhouse and discovered that the lamp emitted physical warmth. Peter was delighted with his treasure, which gave light and warmth and was economical to run.

'That's good husbandry,' he claimed.

I claimed to be tired, and informed Aladdin that this wise virgin was going to bed.

'You seem to have mixed something up,' said Peter.

'Just a few metaphors.' I yawned.

'It's more serious than that,' he said. 'My lamp oil is on the tray where you usually keep olive oil. Are you going to make Virgin Island dressing?'

As summer progressed into blazing heat, we progressed towards the canal summit. Fields of blood red poppies, waving like undulating scarlet carpets in soft breezes, gave way to acre upon acre of sunflowers; grown as a valuable crop, but seen by the casual traveller through France as France's answer to Wordsworth's daffodils. Spying a blaze of yellow that was surely not sunflowers, I discovered, as we drew closer, that it looked like mustard. It may well be the stuff that Dijon is famous for, but to me, it was reminiscent of the fields of rape seen in East Anglia. I mentioned this to Peter, and he said that he could just imagine a dishevelled East Anglian maiden running through the field yelling "Mustard!"

We wondered when we would catch up with the red barge we thought we must be following. We knew it wasn't far ahead because the streaks of red paint on the lock walls were fresh. We knew it must be a barge as wide as Colibri because the paint streaks appeared on both sides of the locks.

It was shortly after we had discovered that waving a frying pan at the radar detector was effective in waking up the one automatic lock between Dijon and the canal summit, that we encountered the perpetrator of the red paint trail. We didn't catch it up, we met it. A double decker barge of almost exactly the same dimensions as the lock it was just leaving. Aptly named Escargot, it crawled towards us at geriatric snail's pace, giving us time to exchange greetings with twenty or so passengers as their deck slowly passed very close to our deck. This was our first sighting of one of several hotel barges carrying anything from four to twenty four American guests, looked after by friendly, cheerful, hardworking crew members from France and Britain, plus some from Australia, New Zealand, Canada and South Africa. United Nations afloat, as it were. As the Escargot passed, videos whirred, cameras clicked, and more pictures of Colibri were recorded on celluloid to be taken to the States.

Photographic equipment on la Reine Pedauque, the next hotel barge we passed, captured a row of my knickers flapping from a washing line outside the wheelhouse door. I could imagine families and friends sitting around in various parts of America in winter, stifling yawns and thinking: Gee, other peoples holiday videos are so boring – and what's with this dame and her knickers anyway?

Eventually we reached Vandenesse. The same autonomous lock instructions were in force. The same leaflets, showing the same little matchstick men gallantly rowing rafts through locks whilst multi-lingual matchstick companions wound handles were offered at the last lock. We put Colibri's ropes on the same bollards that once held Tiger Lily to shore, and cracked open a returnable stared wine bottle at the same log table. It felt like coming home.

Even the weather welcomed us, with clear blue skies and bright sunny days that became hotter and hotter. A bread van that came daily obviated the need to even go cycling in search of a boulangerie. Another mobile shop arrived on the Saturday, selling cheeses and meat. Hoping to buy eggs, I stood in line whilst the van driver exchanged gossip with a little old lady who lived in a house beside the canal. Hearing me ask for eggs, and being told that there were none, the lady offered some from her own hens. As I waited, she went around the garden pushing chickens off nests to collect eggs from beneath them. Six of the biggest, and certainly the freshest, hens eggs I ever saw were presented to me. On the menu, to be eaten at the café-de-log-table that night, was double-yolked egg and chips.

A few boats came and went. Some hire boats, a few yachts passing through to the Mediterranean – we wished them luck and said, 'See you on the way back.' We wondered where to go next, but we were in no particular hurry to go anywhere for a while.

Gazing into the water, I asked Peter if he thought the canal was likely to be very polluted. Before he replied, excited shouts from the opposite bank distracted our attention from pollution. A slightly-built boy, about nine or ten years old, ran along the bank hanging grimly onto a fishing rod that was bent almost double. From the tip of the rod, a line led to beneath Colibri's hull, and we supposed that the boy had caught our propeller. I smiled at the idea of about five stone of boy hauling a hundred tons of barge across the canal and plopping it into his landing net. And he was going to have to land us because his little arms were far too short to describe this one that got away.

Thrashing commotion from our stern wiped the smile from my face as, fascinated, we watched a shape that seemed to be the size of a baby whale being dragged across the canal by a kid that looked more the size to be collecting tadpoles in a jam jar. With assistance from two adult fishermen, who abandoned their own rods in favour of being involved in the monster haul, a huge fish was pulled onto the bank. I was right about one thing, the boy's arms were inadequate to describe this one if it had got away. I asked him to hold the fish so I could take a photograph. With it cradled in his arms, he was able to do so for a few seconds, bony little knees sagging beneath the weight.

'Does that answer your enquiry about pollution?' Peter wanted to know.

Re-assembling my sun bed – which has never been completely stable since Guy stayed the night at Kappelle op den Bos – I went back to my umbrella shaded book.

'See that man?' Peter interrupted my story. 'He must be a Dutchman.'

I looked up to see a guy with a mobile phone looking in our direction and drawing curves in the air with his hand – obviously to assist the listener on the telephone to visualize what he was describing.

'How do you know he's Dutch?' I asked Peter.

'By the way his hand is following the curve of the deck. See, now he's showing how it follows the lines of the hull.'

'Nonsense. He's a Frenchman, describing how my curves follow the lines of the sun bed.'

Yeah, right. The content of that somewhat flimsy conversational exchange seemed to suggest that perhaps we were becoming a little bored. It was probably time to move on and explore some more. But in which direction? We were close to the summit, and had the choice of going back to the River Saone, then choosing which direction to take from there, or going on through the summit tunnel and down the other side of this canal. We were having a summit meeting to decide this tremendously important issue when these people from a sail boat turned up with a bottle of wine. They wanted to invite us for a drink, but thought that we would all be more comfortable on our large deck than on their tiny one. We invited Paul and Penny to join the meeting, and added their wine to the agenda – then our wine, then another one of theirs.

Under Any Other Business, we debated the merits of driving a car to work everyday to earn money versus cruising in poverty. It wasn't a very lively debate; it distinctly lacked the stimulus of well prepared argument. Penny effectively rendered the subject stone dead by asking if anyone knew what day it was. Four people stared blankly into space. By some positive quick thinking, I jumped in after only several seconds of delay with: 'It's either Tuesday or Wednesday.'

'How do you know?' Someone obviously didn't trust me here.

'Because the bread van doesn't come on Mondays. It was either yesterday or the day before that it didn't come, so it must be Tuesday or Wednesday.'

'Damn,' said Penny. 'I was supposed to phone my son on Sunday.'

A statement which jolted my conscience. The last couple of times I had dialled our son's number, I had been treated to yet another recorded message announcing that his mobile phone was out of range. Obviously the tide was low at Woodbridge, and it occurred to me that communication would be assisted if we had a North Sea tide table to hand. Leaving the men discussing engines and water pumps, Penny and I strolled over the bridge to the phone box beside the church. Penny's son wasn't at home so I tried ringing mine.

'Is your son out as well?' asked Penny when I put the phone down.

'Don't know, but the tide is,' I told her.

As we had made the effort of going to the phone box, I called Annie in Belgium. 'If I come from Brussels by train, where can you pick me up?' she asked.

'Dijon,' I told her. 'The station is only ten minutes walk from the port.'

Returning to Colibri, I said to Peter, 'You know that discussion we had trouble in having, about where to go next? Well, we're going back to Dijon.'

The canal and surrounding scenery looks different facing the other way. Downstream cruising reveals bits that are missed on the upward journey. It wasn't simply a case of going back the way we had come, it was more like a new route. Thanks, Annie, we could have missed this by going on over the summit.

Dijon Port was blisteringly hot. As soon as Annie boarded, we slipped ropes and made for some shade. Trees at Plombieres didn't shade the boat, but we were able to sit beneath them until the sun sank behind a hill.

It was nice to have a guest on board. We were anxious to show her the Ouche Valley in the few days she had with us. The uninvited guests who stole the bikes off the aft roof whilst we slept, shocked us from our mellow complacency for a while.

Our own fault maybe; we had never bothered to lock the bikes. Well, they were hardly expensive multi-geared BMX mountain steeds that were likely to attract burglars. They were trusty, rusty and gearless jobs of no lucrative value. Peter decided to talk with the nearby lock keeper before doing anything like notifying the police. This was a minor crime in a small village, so maybe it could be dealt with locally.

Apparently, this sort of minor crime was common here. Not as a general rule, but as a recent result of one small group of local lads. The villagers had stopped reporting offences because, anyone who did so, became a victim of slashed car tyres or broken house windows. Peter was, therefore, encouraged to report the incident to the local gendamerie on the basis that, being non local, he wouldn't be victimised.

A good enough theory. We could be instrumental in ridding the village of its trouble makers, then just move on out of harm's way, but I wasn't too sure about this. I didn't feel public spirited enough to put Colibri at risk if we ever returned to Plombieres. Even if we moved on, all some one needed to do was pinch a couple of bikes and cycle down the towpath to find us.

I raised this worry to the gendarme who had appeared in a big blue van. He was in the process of persuading Peter to submit a formal statement, but he was aware that Peter was hesitating because of my concern. We were reassured that our formal complaint was all the police needed to nail the little sods. They knew who they were, but were powerless to act in the absence of an officially registered complaint. Confident that, with our cooperation, he could remove the culprits, he was equally confident that we would not be exposed to any danger.

Meanwhile, a big blue van parked on the towpath beside our barge was blatantly advertising the fact that we had involved the law. If we didn't assist in the removal of the petty criminals, we were likely to be got at anyway.

I was anxious to leave – as in immediately – and we told the gendarme we would return and pass through, very briefly, around noon on Sunday, when Annie had to be delivered back to Dijon to catch a return train to Brussels.

Shrugging off this unfortunate incident, we cruised on and

enjoyed showing off our little bit of heaven. Annie was an extremely receptive audience and an enthusiastic lock gate operator.

Finding an area of canal wide enough to turn Colibri round, we headed back towards Dijon when it was close to the time for Annie's departure. At approximately eleven forty five on Sunday, we rounded a bend above Plombieres – and sighted a big blue van at the lock. As we approached, the van left the lock and slowly drove along the towpath towards us.

'They are bringing back your bikes!' squealed Annie excitedly.

Behind the crawling police van, a retinue of people and bikes, came into view. Before the van reached us, the widely grinning face of our gendarme could be seen through the windscreen.

'We have your bikes!' a jubilant gendarme called.

'Thank you,' I called back. 'But the red one is not ours.'

I felt really rotten about wiping the smile from his face. With a heavy scowl, he jumped out of the van and demanded to be told where they had pinched that one from, before picking up the alien bike and throwing it into the van. There was an indignant note to the youths' explanation that the bike they took from us had been stolen from them outside a bar in Dijon, so they'd taken another one in order to get home.

Curious, we asked how they had managed to board the barge and remove our bikes without disturbing us. The nonchalant reply that we had made it easy for them by leaving the gangplank down seemed to suggest that this was all our fault really.

A conference with the three youthful culprits, the mother of one that was a minor and the gendarme, resulted in an agreement that, if the lads paid us for the missing bike, we would drop our charge against them. This would put us in the clear, the gendarme explained. There would be no quarrel with us; once the money was received for the other bike, we would be free to travel on with easy minds. The police would then press their own charges. They had been after these lads for some time, and we had been instrumental in providing a vehicle for their arrest, not to mention two rusty ones for their tow path joy ride.

I wasn't at all sure that my mind *was* completely at ease after the exchange between Peter and the gypsy youth. He was the one who handed over the franc notes and, as he did so, he spat on the ground. When Peter took the notes and spat on the ground, the lad looked up sharply and his eyes widened in what looked like fright; showing the first indication that he was in any way concerned about anything.

'Yes,' Peter told him. 'I know your customs. I am a traveller too, and you have offended one of your own kind.'

I felt this interchange had either secured our protection for ever, or set us up for a bundle of future trouble. Either way, we got the hell out of there and spent the night in Dijon.

Annie departed, grumbling about leaving us cruising in glorious weather on the French Canals whilst she must return to work in an office in Brussels. We agreed it was tough, but as we had to do it, we may as well continue the way we were facing and make our way back to the River Saone. Maybe to Macon, or maybe we would turn into the Canal du Centre at Chalon sur Saone and investigate the Loire Valley. Maybe we would just drift and see where our drifting took us.

September brought relief from the heat of August, warm gentle days and a few dull rainy ones. We drifted through clear river water and spent starlit nights in a haze of red wine and barbecue smoke.

Returning with Brian from his customary evening walk along the river bank, I thought I heard a telephone. A bottle of red Villages, bought in Macon, had accompanied our meal. I was used to less heady wine, so I just shook my head to clear it of fanciful sounds. I knew I couldn't be hearing a telephone.

'I can hear a telephone,' I told Peter a few minutes later.

'Don't be daft, there's not a house for miles.'

This was true. There wasn't anything for miles, except fields, trees and river. I shrugged and moved the supper plates aside so Peter could put his oil lamp on the deck table. When I heard the phone again, I said nothing.

'Car phone, perhaps?' said Peter.

I was relieved – he'd heard it too. At least, if I was going ga-ga, he was coming with me. When Dillon called: 'It's for you-hoo,' that settled it. If I was going on a loopy trip, either I was taking a parrot along with me or there was definitely a phone ringing somewhere. The absence of a road, or even a track, ruled out Peter's car phone theory. So where on earth. . .

'It's coming from that tree!'

I was glad I hadn't said that one.

When the tree rang again, Dillon said: 'Hello. Who's it for?'

It must have been Storm's ear-splitting squawk that startled it. With a rustle of leaves, leaving a swaying branch behind, a feathered trim phone flew off into the dusk on a long distance call.

The telephone bird had stirred dormant chords in Dillon's memory. She relived the plug-in-switch-on civilization era when she used to delight in copying our telephone, and I used to curse about running to answer a ringing parrot. We were subjected to a part of Dillon's repertoire that we hadn't heard for two or three years. Then it had been a set piece: Three rings – Hello – Who's it for? – It's for yoo-hoo. However, intervening events had influenced her, and now it was often for Brian or Pee-ter. One time, three rings were followed by: Oh shit! It was a briefly recaptured phase, and it made a change from living with a parrot that thought it was a circular saw or an electric drill.

The walnut that fell on my head and bounced across the deck woke us up to the fact that Autumn had arrived. That night, the weather changed. We lay in bed listening to wind whistling through trees, water slapping against the hull and walnuts bombarding the roof. It sounded as if we were under attack from some hidden enemy.

Next morning the sun shone again, but we knew it couldn't last. Laughing at Brian chasing nuts across the deck, we collected our thoughts as well as a potato net of walnuts. It was time to seriously consider where we would spend winter.

Chapter Thirteen

FROM HERE TO – WHERE?

Late October. The Canal du Bourgogne will be closing its gates next month and the lock keepers will get on with their winter lives until March. We have time for a leisurely cruise through the Ouche Valley before we coil our ropes and settle down for winter. The valley is at it's most beautiful at this time of year. The sight of trees in their Autumn colours on the canal bank and hillside beyond make my throat ache.

Peter is cooking supper on a bed of wood beside me; maybe our last barbecue this year. Wood smoke curls up and mingles with a canopy of bronze and gold above our heads. The little River Ouche flows gently before us, and the evening sun casts a mellow glow on our home in the canal behind. Soon the water will turn pink, then red, as it reflects another beautiful sunset. We will snuggle into warm jumpers, light the hurricane lamp, and sit by the glow of dying wood embers until it becomes too chilly to sit on the bank.

Soon, we would turn round and make our way back to St. Jean de Losne, where we had elected to spend winter. A pleasant, friendly town, with all the shops we required and the company of other live aboard boaters. Meanwhile, Fleurey was a good place to enjoy some tranquillity.

Some American visitors, taking a late cruise on Escargot, strolled along the towpath. Why were we moving our barge along by ropes? they wanted to know. Had the engine broken down? We explained that I had asked for a slightly different view. By moving a few feet, we could see a pretty hillside more clearly through the trees. They were fascinated by the idea of simply moving a home to get a better view from the window. In fact, they were fascinated by the whole idea of anyone living on a barge, and as they hadn't time to qualify for the ten minutes of questions rule, we invited them to see our home. After exclaiming over everything, they sat on our deck and waved at their fellow guests floating past on Escargot.

'We have plenty of time to catch them up,' said the one called

Ethel. 'That barge moves so slowly. Isn't it just great to move so slowly?'

We agreed that it certainly was, and that we had improved our quality of life by adopting a snail's pace. The two men, who were taking a cruise because they had both suffered heart attacks, were in favour of this approach to life.

'You should write a book,' they said. Sure, we'd heard this a few times before.

'In winter, when you have nothing to do.'

This was a new one – we should have time to write a book in winter!

What was this *nothing to do in winter* story that people put about anyway? This winter, we only had to build a third bedroom complete with shower room, convert Pieter the Plank's planks into a front door and a dining table, build a bookcase to relieve cardboard boxes of books and do something about the fact that the fireplace still needs a mantlepiece. Not to mention the act of turning the aft quarters into a cosy self-contained nest. The operatically ornate stove still stood behind a heap of nail-encrusted precious teak, waiting to be installed. Meanwhile, its mountains were capped with cobwebs and there was enough drifting dust on the shelf-like bosom of the full-chested lady to dampen any tenor's aria.

By mid-November, we conceded that the summer cruising season was over. The vibrant brightness of October had deteriorated into greyish November days. Early morning mist, suspended over the canal, often stretched it's privilege to lunch time. The Bourgogne locks were closing for winter, except for the one that led from the canal to the river at St. Jean de Losne. Knowing this afforded freedom to travel if the weather tempted us onto the river during winter, we placed Colibri alongside the bank in the Port of St. Jean, with a lock comfortingly between us and a river that – so we were told – could erupt in a spate of flood. We had only seen the Saone as a gentle lady; even this late in the year, she flowed serenely on her way to meet the mighty Rhone at Lyon. But we had reason to believe in stories of rivers in heavy flood.

Summer cruising boats were being laid up; their owners packing to return to wherever home was. Addresses and *see you next year* promises were exchanged. We promised Evangeline and

Roger that we would keep an eye on their boat, and we already looked forward to their return, and that of liveaboards, Bill and Frances, who were taking their gorgeous tjalk through the still open Canal du Centre to spend winter in Paris.

Most other full time liveaboards had already settled into semi-permanent winter moorings. Mike was preparing his handsome tjalk for the family to take up full time residence. As if it was a rather odd thing to do, I asked why he was living in France on a barge. He replied, 'There I was, sitting in my car as usual at eight-thirty in the morning, queuing up with a hundred and one other cars to take my turn round the Colchester/Ipswich Road roundabout, and it suddenly occurred to me that there had to be more to life than this.'

'I know that bloody roundabout!' I exclaimed. We'd found a fellow Ipswichian.

The mooring Tony and Catherine took was at an island. When they invited us to dinner, we were not too sure how we would get to their barge.

'I'll motor the dinghy across, and we'll rendezvous at nineteen hundred hours,' Tony informed us.

We were in position at the appointed hour, and we heard the phut phut of a seagull engine approaching. I have always had an innate mistrust of any piece of machinery that requires a bit of string to start it; be it a lawn mower, a chain saw or an outboard motor. It's not only the fact that I have never managed to master the flick of wrist and sharp elbow jerk necessary to start these things, my main fear of outboard dinghy motors is engendered by my knowledge that it is essential to change from drive forward gear to neutral just prior to the landing target being reached – and timing is critical. Then there is this sneaky little habit they have of dying, for no apparent reason, somewhere between ship and shore. I had fond memories of Tiger Lily and her Zodiac dinghy, but my memories of the Zodiac's outboard Seagull brought on shudders equalled only by the shudders evoked by memories of a certain little diesel heater that I had never learned to live with.

'Cutting engine now,' called Tony, when he and his dinghy were a few feet from where we stood. 'Be ready to grab the dinghy as soon as it makes contact with land.'

With water lapping over the top of only one wellie, Peter

managed a successful grab, and the wooden dinghy was alongside. I was fed into it and ordered to hang on to Tony's shoulders whilst Peter's weight was added to a bobbing craft that leaned at an alarming angle. Redistribution of body weight was then called upon to enable the propeller to reach the water. As it happened, the Seagull behaved perfectly and delivered us safely to Tony's barge. Stepping over it to alight, I patted the gallant little motor's fly wheel in approval. It spat two stroke oil at me.

It was a first for us. Never before had we taken a Seagull-propelled conveyance to a dinner party of such elegance dressed in wellies and oilskins. Damp jeans and thick, knee-high fisherman's socks were tucked beneath a rich cherrywood table. Light from a candelabra danced on family silver and crystal glass of a highly respectable age. From a lofty position on an oak panelled wall, an ancestral accredited boar's head surveyed a delicious, several course gourmet meal, served by a gracious host dressed in oil-stained corduroy trousers, a checked lumberjack shirt and a bow tie.

Taking into account our less than compos mentis state when we climbed into the dinghy for the return journey, Tony responsibly allocated crew duties. One person would pull the cord, one would hang onto the tiller and the other would push the dinghy off from the side of the barge.

'Don't push of until. . .'

Too late. With an exuberance born of quite a lot of white Chardonay, red Corbierres and crystal-decanted port, I pushed off before the pull cord monitor had located the notch in the fly wheel. Again, the gallant little motor behaved well; responding to the third pull.

It wasn't until the cloud of thick black smoke dispersed that we were able to ascertain the density of the fog that had descended whilst we ate. Meanwhile, our attention had been focused on the starting of the engine – with no one paying attention to which direction we faced after my premature shove had launched us into a spin. We moved in the general direction of a blur of land-based lights.

This particular Seagull did not, in fact, boast two gear situations. Neutral was not part of its act. The only way to actually stop propulsion was to stop the engine. The engine was cut six feet from a wooden landing stage. The dinghy drifted five feet. We would probably have made it if two people had not stood up at the same time to lunge for the wooden landing stage. My grasp on the landing stage prevented the dinghy from rolling over but, for the second time that night, I pushed when I shouldn't have. None of three pairs of flailing arms succeeded in bridging the now five foot gap between us and one wooden landing stage. Nothing for it but to restart the Seagull which, I was not surprised to discover, was related to our rotten little diesel heater. Breaths were held in suspense and against clouds of black smoke. Would the next cough result in an actual firing of engine? We drifted, as frantic cord-flicking wrists became certain candidates for plaster casts.

It was whilst we all had our heads down, searching for a broken pull cord amongst three pairs of wellied feet, that a wooden landing stage came up and hit us.

We waited until Tony had been swallowed up by the fog, and Catherine's voice could be heard in muffled response to his call for directions, then set off to find our own barge.

It seemed odd to stay still in one place after our summer of exploring. I rather missed the summer tourists and the chance encounters with people who were interested enough to ask all those questions about our barge, ourselves and our lifestyle. Funny that; if strangers had come into our garden in England and walked around staring at our cottage before firing personal questions at us, we would have resented the intrusion. In fact, we would have considered it a damn cheek.

But the inquisition party didn't all leave with the summer. The member for Birmingham appeared from under our boat one frosty afternoon. Seeing a pair of upturned, highly polished leather shoes on the bank, I looked over the side to see that they were attached to a slightly mud-stained pair of khaki legs. Leaning further over the side, I enquired of a khaki bum: 'Is there something I can do for you?' This obviously startled the owner of the bum because he raised his head sharply and clunked it on the underside of the counter-stern.

'I was just looking at your rudder,' I was offered by way of explanation of the fact that I had found a man under my home. 'Is this your barge? Must be Dutch.'

'Yes, It's Dutch. A luxe motor actually,' I proudly replied.

'Yes, it could be, it has the look of a luxe motor. Where did you get it, Holland?'

'Yep. That's the place to buy Dutch luxe motors.'

'Not necessarily, it's possible to find them elsewhere. What size is this thing?'

'Eighty seven foot.'

'Are you sure? I would have put it at about eighty.'

'Eighty seven,' I repeated, 'with a sixteen foot six inch beam.'

'Really? Sixteen foot six? Unusual that, more likely to be around fifteen foot. Where was it built?'

'Sneek.'

'Didn't think they made them there. Did you bring it from Sneek?'

'No, Leeuwarden.

'Oh yeah? Which route did you take?'

'Harlingen, Ijsselmeer, Markermeer, Amster. . .'

'I doubt you would've come that way, love. You would have had a bit of bother at sea in a barge.'

'Not really, this one has a keel.'

'Are you sure? Barges don't usually have keels.'

'This one was built as a coaster. It has a keel.'

'Uhuh? What engine's she got?'

I was ready for this one. I had been asked that question so often that, 'Ask Peter,' had become a boring reply, so I learned the details off by heart. Although it meant little to me, I reeled off: 'DAF turbo six cylinder diesel water cooled.'

'You sure it's water cooled?'

Yes, I was sure – as I was about the draft – air height – displacement.

'Hydraulic steering, of course.' Was he asking or telling me?

'No, not hydraulic. Chain steering, actually. – Yes, I am sure. Chain steering it is.'

This was getting tedious. Where was Peter? Why didn't he come forward to help me out? I looked around hopefully and caught a glimpse of Peter in the wheelhouse just before he quickly ducked out of sight. Not quickly enough; I had seen the grin on his face.

'What sort of speed does she do?' was the next question.

'Oh, you know, up to about fifteen knots.'

'Ah yes,' came the reply. 'Around fifteen knots max would be the norm.'

I'd cracked it! The way to stop this man doubting my every word was to precede my answers with: You know.

'When was she built?'

'You know, early thirties.'

'Are you sure? That would make her over sixty-years-old.'

'Yup.'

'Is there a generator on board?'

'Oh yes, I'm sure we've got one of those. It's a Mitsubishi diesel, 10 kw max, 6 kw continuous, single phase, 220 volt output – I think.'

A pause whilst he either digests this information or the fact that I've given this information. A slight shake of head of the *is she sure she knows what she's talking about* type before the next question.

'What thickness of steel is it?'

'I don't know. It's just a Mitsubishi 10 kw. . .'

'No, the hull. What thickness steel?'

'Iron actually, 8mm.'

'Iron? Are you sure? They usually build out of 6mm steel.'

I'd had enough of this!

'Belgian and French peniche, maybe,' I answered. 'But this baby is an 8mm thick iron, sixty-yearold, eighty-seven by sixteen foot six Dutch luxe motor built in Sneek with a keel and. . .'

I realized I was being rude. This man was probably a very nice person; not really someone who was trying to catch me out, or prove that he knew more about my barge than I did. He was giving up his time – a lot of his time – to talk to me, and was displaying a flattering interest in my lovely boat. We like that, it makes us feel good. Yes, this was a really nice man. The problem was – and this was not this nice guy's fault – I had more or less exhausted my fund of technical knowledge. I smiled charmingly and waited for the next question. If I didn't know the answer, I would make one up. This plonker didn't believe a word I said anyway!

He stayed – or rather outstayed – the course and, with admirable stamina, more than qualified for the *Ten minutes asking questions, invite on board* rule. After a further fifteen minutes, I asked him if he would like to come on board for a drink.

'Are you sure?' was the inevitable reply.

'Sure I'm sure,' I told him. 'After all, the arm is over the sun yard.'

'Er . . . are you sure you've got that right?'

'Certainly. I know all about the yard being over the arm sun, it's the same thing as six o'clock G'n'T. Do come on board and meet my husband. He'll tell you all about the curtains and matching chair covers.'

I knew he was gobsmacked when he walked through the front door because he stared, open-mouthed, and didn't proffer a single question in the twenty seconds it took for Peter to put a beer in his hand. A quick gulp of beer resurrected his sagging lower jaw, and he asked, 'Did you do all this yourself?'

'Not really, Peter helped me a bit,' I replied modestly.

'Why don't you. . .'

'Your ball,' I told Peter as I went to pour myself a glass of wine.

' . . . write a book about all your experiences?'

I smiled wryly to myself and thought: Ho, ho, ho! What is it with these jokers who think I've got time to write a book?

I had no intention of writing a book. But then, I'd had no intention of going to Belgium either. Anyway, I've read about people writing books – usually in books about people writing books. They say things like:

He sat down at his Smith Corona and typed Chapter one, then stared at the blank page, inspiration deserting him.

Or: *Cynthia ripped the page out of the Olivetti, screwed it into a ball and threw it across the room at the overflowing wastepaper basket.*

I've often wondered why these Cynthia types didn't keep a waste paper basket beside their typing chair, and why they didn't realize that, if they didn't screw the pages into balls, the basket wouldn't fill up so quickly. Obviously there is less dramatic frustrational outlet in neatly filing rejected pages in an easy to reach receptacle. And, I mean, do real people really decide: I'm going to write a book today, then sit at a typewriter, type page one and realize they don't have a book to write?

Thinking that some day, somewhere, I may find time to write an article, and being reluctant to risk the blank page, screwed up, missed basket Cynthia syndrome, I began to scribble notes on the *Building materials to buy* pad in the kitchen. Rushing to a smoke-belching grill in the middle of page seven, I thought: You can't write an article without burning a bit of toast. I scribbled this profound thought under *size 8 screws and polyurethane varnish.*

'Burnt toast again!' said Peter, scraping charcoal onto the side of his plate.

'You can't write an article without burning a bit of toast,' I retorted.

'Very profound!' he responded, cementing over the holes with marmalade, 'Why have I got a cup of hot water?'

'Bugger! I forgot to put the coffee in.'

'Meg, may I make a formal request that you do your writing *after* meals?'

'Thank you, Peter, I accept your formal offer to wash up.'

I put a scribble pad of my own in the cutlery drawer after the day Peter came home from shopping, I asked him if he got everything, and he replied, 'Not quite, the Do It Yourself shop was fresh out of *It was dark when we moored up under the trees.*

Peter bought me an electric typewriter for Christmas. I bought Peter a 220 volt inverter so I could run my typewriter from the ship's batteries.

A friend popped in and found me standing at the typewriter in paint-smeared overalls, poking at the keys with a tile-grouted finger.

'What are you doing?' she asked.

'Writing a bloody book – I can't keep it short enough to be an article!'

When we invited Catherine and Tony to have dinner with us, it was obviously going to be simpler – for us – than going to their place. All I had to cope with was cooking a meal in my own convenient kitchen, then, full of good food, sated with wine and replete with enjoyable conversation, toddle off to the comfort of my cosy bedroom. And that's just how it was – until the door entered the proceedings.

Tony and Cat arrived early; their barge was cold and they were well acquainted with Colibri's warmth. Exclaiming at the heat from our wood burner, Tony defrosted his hands before we sat down to eat and to discuss many things. The topic over the cheese course was how damn cold it was on Tony and Cat's barge. By the time the camembert, roquefort and brie had been demolished, it had been unanimously agreed that far too much heat was lost through their wheelhouse.

'What we need is a door,' Tony said. 'But it's difficult to come up with something that is suitably old and in keeping with the boat's decor.'

Being more an advocate of comfort than a connoisseur of doors, Cat declared that she was likely to shiver all winter whilst Tony searched for an appropriate lump of wood.

Peter's question, 'Would a sixty-year-old teak door with a leaded stained glass panel be considered appropriate?' had Tony practically salivating.

It just needed me to agree that we didn't really have use for all four of the original aft quarters doors, and Peter and Tony were off on a treasure hunt. Taking our wine glasses with us, Cat and I adjourned to the lounge and settled down for a natter by the fire.

'Where's the electric drill?' Peter returned to ask.

'How on earth would I know?' I replied.

'You were the last one to use it.'

'Quite likely, but it's after midnight,' I retorted. 'I don't do tools at this time of night.'

The elusive tool was obviously found because, a few noisy minutes later, the two men re-appeared carrying a door. The coffee table was cleared, the door was laid tenderly across it, the generator start switch was clicked and, in the early hours of morning, emergency surgery was carried out with a circular saw. Orange dust spurted into the air and spilled onto the carpet as the bottom of an appropriate teak door was amputated to an appropriate size. Some final swipes with the electric plane were executed with a triumphant flourish, Cat made some erratic swipes at the carpet with an apparently uncontrollable hoover, and our dinner guests departed to convey their trophy to their island by dinghy.

It wasn't until I went to bed that I discovered our bedroom door had gone.

Burrowed under the duvet, shivering and cursing about the icy draught that whistled from the wheelhouse into the bedroom, I refrained from politely listening to Peter's explanation that it had been easier to take our bedroom door off it's hinges than to unearth one of the unused ones from under the debris in the aft quarters in the dark.

I broke my silence at breakfast next day by announcing, 'Of course, you do realize that Tony's slopes the wrong way.'

I beg your pardon!' came indistinctly through a mouthful of lightly tanned toast.

'The stained glass panel,' I patiently explained. 'To follow the curve of their ceiling, they need a right sloping glass panel. Our bedroom door was carefully selected for the fact that the panel slopes to the left.'

'That is very clear thinking considering the amount of wine we consumed last night,' my husband commented.

'Not at all,' I scathingly replied. 'I do sleep on the side nearest to the gap where there used to be a door you know. I had a refreshingly icy draught piercing my head all night.'

Determined to finish the building work, we launched an all out attack on the aft quarters. It was important to install the little iron stove as we needed somewhere warm to set up a work bench. By working ten hours or so a day, we had cleared, insulated, ceilinged and walled the aft area within two weeks.

Peter was working on the new front door when I asked him if he was ready for a drink. 'Is it wine o'clock already?' he asked. After un-earthing and consulting a clock, I informed him that it was twenty past wine and I was exhausted.

It was then that we made a rule that we should slow down, stop work at six in the evenings and have a day off each week. A neighbour was surprised to find us next day, with our feet up in front of the fire, reading swapped paperbacks at eleven in the morning. 'What happened?' asked the visitor. 'I've never seen you two taking it easy before.'

'We're having a Sunday,' I said.

'But it's Tuesday today,' she pointed out.

'So, it's Sunday the Tuesdayth. Would you like some coffee?'

'And that's another first. I've never been on this boat before and been offered coffee,' said our visitor. 'Did you run out of wine as well as things to do?'

That's the trouble with France, there's all that good cheap wine and it always seems so much easier to open a bottle than to put the kettle on. It's a bit like a mountaineer being asked why he feels compelled to climb Everest and he answers: Because it's there. I say the same thing when anyone asks why we drink so much wine.

Likewise, why do we feel we must explore another canal? Quite simply, because it's there.

The beautiful River Saone was there – just beyond one lock. After staying moored in one place for two months, we felt the urge to move onto the river for a while. Five foot long heavy iron stakes, banged well into the bank, gave a secure river mooring in an idyllic setting. A one-winged lone swan adopted us and came daily to bang on the hull and demand bread.

Brian much preferred it here. Always inhibited by the presence of other people, he enjoyed our relaxed evening strolls along the unpeopled river bank. We enjoyed looking at the moon reflected in the river on clear cold nights and the sun sparkling on water on cold bright days.

Then the rain came. And it came, and it came. The River locks were closed, and any ships unfortunate enough to need to travel, had to pass over the lock weirs. Further South, the River Rhone was closed to navigation completely. We heard of a commercial barge that broke free from its mooring and ended up sideways across a bridge, firmly jammed there by the strong current of that mighty river in flood.

We kept a daily eye on the water level as it gradually climbed the three feet of our mooring stakes that protruded from the ground. When it reached the top of the stakes, we seriously considered going back into the canal. But this would mean demounting the wheelhouse. The water level was now too high for us to pass under the bridge to the lock that led into the canal. We procrastinated, not relishing the task of taking the wheelhouse roof off in pouring rain. Surely the rain would stop soon and the river would subside before we became endangered.

The morning we awoke to find the mooring stakes under water, we decided we must make the move the very next day if things became any worse. The stakes were still very firm in the ground and showed no signs of letting us down, but conditions showed no signs of improving.

We made the move that night, when someone came to tell us that the river authorities had issued a warning that they had lost control of the flow at the lock above us. Water levels were expected to rise up to a metre overnight. With the help of our warning friend and his son, we moved into a disused lock, leaving our stakes still firmly embedded in the bank. Positioned mid-lock, we strung ropes to the lock bollards on either side. This was a wide lock, and if we stayed in the middle, we would not be in danger of being caught on the lock walls when the water subsided.

In the morning, we were well above the height of the lock walls. For three days, Brian was marooned on board with sanitary arrangements courtesy of building sand in a cardboard box, and we waded down the gang plank in wellies.

Fourteen feet and rising is the best way I can think of to describe Bella. If any normal dog leaves a muddy bank and walks across a deck, it leaves neat patterns of sets of four paw marks. But then, no one has ever tried to claim that Bella is a normal dog. When she crosses our white painted deck, she leaves enough muddy paw prints to suggest that a fourteen footed, demented weasel has run amok. This in itself is odd because she seems to spend eighty per cent of the time in the air.

We were asked to look after Bella whilst her people went to England for a few days. She was delivered to us with a shredded blanket, a distorted plastic food bowl, a pack of food and some instructions: Don't leave her at home on her own, she'll wreck the boat.

'Okay. If I need to go shopping, I'll take her with me.' I said.

'Whatever you do, don't leave her in your jeep – she'll eat it.'

I looked down at about thirteen inches of poodle. Bella squinted cutely up at me through her Sue Ellen fringe. 'She'll be fine,' I assured her anxious owners. 'When will you be back?'

'Around ten o'clock Thursday morning. By the way, try to keep her in for a few hours after we leave – she chases cars.'

As soon as her people had stepped off the boat, Bella attempted to claw her way through our front door. We placed a sheet of plywood firmly across the door. Bella stood, head on one side, and watched from three feet away. She then leapt into the air, curled up into a quivering ball and threw herself at the plywood. A dozen or so times, she bounced off and launched herself again.

'She'll soon get tired,' Peter announced. 'She's very small to expend that amount of energy for any length of time.'

She showed no sign of tiring. In fact, her energy spring was winding up into an ever tighter coil. I held her down and tried to soothe her. That was when the whining started, followed by the howling. Three hours later, the parrots were whining and howling. Unable to stand the cacophony in stereo, we let Bella out. She stood at the bow and barked at a fisherman. When the fisherman packed his rods and left, I threw Bella off the boat. She stood on the bank and barked at the boat.

Bella was our guest for four nights. Bella is not big on sleeping at night. At ten o'clock Thursday morning, I was at the bow of the barge looking out for the soonest sighting of Bella's owners' car.

At twelve o'clock, we were in danger of slipping into panic mode. At One o'clock, I just knew that we were stuck with a miniature canine disaster whilst her owners spent weeks in a hospital somewhere between here and Calais recovering from a road accident. I just knew I was going to rocket the sale of Vallium into a new world record – the marketing manager's felt tip pen would shoot off the edge of his sales chart.

Of course we understood that Bella's master had the sense to pull off road to have a kip for a couple of hours. It certainly doesn't make sense for a man, tired from travelling all night, to continue to drive on a busy motorway in wintry conditions. We were so very happy to see him safely back – and we didn't mind in the least that his dog was ecstatic to be taken away.

So, we were left in peace with two whining parrots, and whenever Bella is brought to see us, her fourteen feet leave the ground and she hurls herself at us in an *I'm so pleased to see you* assault. Little bitch.

Spring seemed to jump out of nowhere at the end of February. It was time to work outside. Time to paint the foredeck, to rub down and varnish exterior woodwork, to sit on deck and enjoy the sunshine.

Time to acknowledge that – for the second time – our year of freedom was almost up and we must make plans.

Back in St Jean port, we were doing the sit on deck bit, aware that we were procrastinating over the making plans issue, when Peter suddenly asked me what I would like for my birthday this year.

'Well, let's see,' I said. 'In recent years, I've had a chain saw, a rope, a ladder, a ratchet screwdriver. Last year, I had the best present ever. Last year, on my birthday, we set out on our year of freedom. What are you offering this year?'

At that moment, a voice hailed us from a deck across the water. 'Hey, you two. If you've nothing better to do than sit in the sun, you'd better join us for a drink.'

Walking over the bridge to join our friends, we admitted that it was rather difficult to concentrate on our future plans whilst the distraction of other carefree boaters was all around. We had moved back into the Port of St. Jean de Losne when people began to return from winter absence. Some came by car or train to reclaim and re-float laid up boats, others came by boat from their winter moorings elsewhere. We happily welcomed back friends of last year and greeted new ones. Steve and Hil sailed into port just as we were leaving for the *Chez Thierey* restaurant.

Eighteen of us sat down at the long table Thierey had assembled on the occasion of Mac's birthday. The fact that most of us didn't know who Mac was didn't seem important. In fact, I only recognised a handful of the people present, and I'd certainly never met the guy on my left. I chatted with this interesting American who had sailed his yacht across the Atlantic. Nodding towards the lady across the table, who had entered the restaurant with him, I asked if his wife enjoyed sea sailing.

'I guess so,' he replied rather oddly.

'I'm sorry,' I hastily said. 'That was crass of me, perhaps you aren't married?'

'Oh yeah, we're married all right. Not to each other, but we're married.'

He had addressed me by name a few times, so I thought I should ask his name.

'I'm Mac,' he said.

'Happy birthday,' I said. 'I'm enjoying your party.' I also told him that, if he was Mac, then I did happen to know that the lovely lady across the table was indeed his wife.

'Sure,' he remarked. 'But she's gonna divorce me when I donate our boat to Mother Teresa.'

During the course of the evening, it was proposed that we all get together for a barbecue next day. Somehow or other, it was decided that this would take place on Colibri. Something to do with it being the only boat big enough to accommodate more than a dozen people.

It was a flaccid drapeau sort of day. Thick syrupy heat hung heavily in the still air, and lunchtime brie and Aligote hung heavily on us. St Jean port lay beneath a torpor of post Sunday lunch inertia. A few bodies languished damply beneath deck awnings, but there was no sign of what could be described as life. A fan assisted siesta to recharge our batteries before receiving barbecue guests was voted.

Through a semi-comatose state induced by the soporific droning of the fan, I thought I dreamed the distant voices calling our names. The sharp clank of our boarding ladder pierced nebulous layers of sleep, and full consciousness arrived with the clink of bottles. Footsteps on the side deck had us scrambling out of bed and reaching for clothes.

By the time our visitors arrived at the front door, I was wearing a back-to-front caftan, and Peter was wearing a nonchalant grin and my shorts. Knowing that Peter hadn't had time to find his underpants, I shot a brief – pardon the pun – glance in his direction. As I feared, one more step and all would be revealed. I'm not boasting about my husband, it's just that the legs of my shorts are very short. Speedily positioning myself between Peter and the visitors, I said, 'Darling, why don't you go and slip into something more comfortable BEFORE YOU SIT DOWN?'

Notwithstanding a rude awakening by barbecue enthusiasts arriving two hours early, we had a super evening in great company. My role as hostess was played out by me chatting and laughing with a bunch of fun people while a Texan called Bee-ill and an ex British Airways pilot known as Roger Roger handled the cooking. Frances – in a pinafore bearing the words: *Who invited all these tacky people* – proved to be a much better deckside caterer than I am.

This particularly enjoyable evening made it so much harder to come to terms with the fact that, whilst all these happy people were planning their summer cruises, our year of freedom had reached an end. We knew that, in order to sensibly plan our next step in life, we must remove ourselves from the influence of this delightful bunch of carefree boaters. A quiet mooring to a deserted bank on the river seemed likely to be the best place to collect our wayward thoughts.

Calling in to say goodbye to a neighbouring barge, we stopped long enough to share a square plastic bottle of extremely palatable *Villageois* red, over which we related the tale of our interrupted siesta. 'Of course,' I said, 'what we need is a siesta flag.'

'You mean a flag that says *sod off we're bonking*,' was suggested. Rather a lot of words to put on a flag, was the general opinion. How about just the initials S.O.W.B.? It was agreed that, if we all had this flag, we could form an elite club. A sort of fraternity of cruising bonkers with branches all over Europe.

This was beginning to sound like serious fun. Another bottle of Chateau Plastique flipped its lid, and we settled down to discuss a club constitution. 'But,' asked a prospective committee member, 'what do we do if strangers ask about the flag?'

This was agendared as a valid question and put to the floor. A solution was proposed: If the stranger was a cruising type, and we felt at ease enough in their company to explain, then they would be the right sort to invite to join the club. If, on the other hand, we felt an explanation would invite disapproval, we would say that the initials stood for Society Of Water Brethren. This was a good let out, as well as being the criterion for enlisting new members for those branches throughout Europe.

Nobody ever did get around to designing or making a flag before everyone sailed off in various directions. So, if you want to join the club, contact Steve. It was his idea – except he wanted to call it the Federation Of Water Folk.

When a library book is overdue, you either take it back and pay the fine, or pretend you've lost it, pay the full cost and continue to enjoy reading. Soon it would be May, and we were already overdue on our borrowed year.

'Are you practising saying w – w – work?' I asked Peter.

'Under my breath, and without enthusiasm. I mean, Meg, how can we go back to normal living?'

'That depends on what you mean by normal,' I replied.

We decided to approach normalcy cautiously by requesting a bank statement to be sent from England. When Poste Restante produced the inevitable window envelope, knowing that it contained a megaphone calling, *Come in number five, your time is up*, I tucked it under a matt black sauce bottle of wild flowers. By unspoken agreement, we left it there until after dinner when, with a fresh litre bottle with stars on, we settled on deck to watch the sun set over the fields. I cautiously opened the envelope whilst Peter fed suppertime bread to the swans.

On the one hand, the envelope contained a pleasant surprise. We were amazed at the small number of French francs we had bought for our living expenses over the year. On the other hand, interest on hard earned money, put to one side to finance our year, had halved – and francs were now costing twenty-five per cent more than when we left Belgium. So, the British Government had megaphones in their window envelopes too!

What to do? Panic and both of us rush out to find work – or acknowledge that, however hard you tried, you couldn't win? We had done all the right things. Peter had worked hard for over thirty years to provide a mortgage for his family and to put something away for a rainy day. Our rainy day had arrived; our home in England had manifested a structural defect, rendering it valueless. Solicitors were currently eroding what was left of our capital. Okay, no one ever promised me roses all my life but, once again, I had the feeling that we were not in control of our own circumstances.

This time, Malcom was nowhere near, and we could hardly blame Radio Monaco either. Government and surveyors maybe, but what's the point? At the end of the day, you are on your own with whatever is dealt to you. Life doesn't come with a rubber stamped guarantee. Sometimes batteries are included, otherwise you buy your own.

St. Jean de Losne is a watershed; an appropriate place to handle a crossroad in your life. So, we'd been dealt a financial crisis – who escapes at least one of those in their life? – but we had just been dealt a beautiful year of freedom as well. The latter didn't cancel out or financially assist the former, but it sure as hell helped to mentally deal with it.

Peter could now return to high pressure work at a noisy, polluted airfield. We could join the queue at the Colchester/Ipswich Road roundabout, awaiting our turn to belt down the A12.

Or we could take one of the five slow lanes out of St. Jean de Losne.

Even a multi-sided ten franc coin is inadequate to cover the multi aspects and complexities of life. Anyway, we were already half way down our second litre and a half of Villageoise red. I wasn't about to toss my coin without the guarantee of being able to catch it. We couldn't afford to lose ten francs. It's worth two litres of wine for heavens sake! At this moment in time, we could still afford to buy our own batteries. We had no way of knowing how long they would last. When they went flat, we would think again.

Leaving a moonlit deck at two in the morning, creeping so as not to disturb the swans, we went to bed with peaceful minds. Sod the rainy day – our faith was in the sunny summer within our grasp.

My five franc share of red wine dissolved into a dream in which I reclined on the deck of a barge that was drifting gently down the Rhone towards the South of France. Beside me, on a collapsed sunbed surrounded by concrete slabs, Malcom sat with a case of baby oil on his lap.

EPILOGUE

Not only have I enjoyed re-living the Colibri story, it has taken me beyond being a two finger typist. When I first began committing my disjointed scribblings to print, my typing skills were such that, when typing "floppy disk" in chapter four, I typed in a C where an S should have been. Leaving an R out of "paper work" gave me a paper wok. This tendency of mine to mistype does seem to produce some singularly unuseful objects! I now have profound sympathy for a friend with a spelling hang up who had an extra D in his rigid.

The sail off into the sunset conclusion to chapter thirteen was, for us, an end of a mental attitude and the beginning of a new phase in our lives. We went on to explore France by river and canal, but we somehow always ended up back on the Canal du Bourgogne; spending our winter months moored beneath the medieval hill-top village of Chateauneuf-en-Auxois.

During the fifteen years Colibri was our home, we saw many changes. Not the least being the advent of the GSM phone. We bought, at huge expense, one of the first thousand Motorola produced in Germany. It was the size of two house bricks and, although we had one of the earliest French SIM cards, it was a few years before a signal could be found in many areas. We later became the first people in France to receive and send fax via a computer and mobile phone, some years before email even came into being.

Peter never did return to the noise, pollution and stress of an international airport. Instead, the obvious answer to how we were going to fend off those dreaded window envelopes from the bank was for us to operate Colibri as a charter cruise barge. That way we were able to continue to live on the waterways of France as well as share our knowledge of and passion for the lifestyle we had chosen for ourselves.

Some of the people we have enjoyed on board have given me fuel for that article I may find time to write one day. I started jotting notes on the kitchen menu pad, and Peter asked only recently if I was planning to serve cream or lemon sauce with: *She left her false teeth on the anchor winch.*

Mary Cassells - 2009

Printed in Great Britain
by Amazon.co.uk, Ltd.,
Marston Gate.